OXFORD LEARNER'S POCKET

Phrasal Verbs & Idioms

Ruth Gairns and
Stuart Redman

Great Clarendon Street, Oxford, OX2 6DP, United Kingdom

Oxford University Press is a department of the University of Oxford. It furthers the University's objective of excellence in research, scholarship, and education by publishing worldwide. Oxford is a registered trade mark of Oxford University Press in the UK and in certain other countries

First published in 2013
2017 2016
10 9 8

ISBN: 978 0 19 432549 3

Printed in China

This book is printed on paper from certified and well-managed sources

Contents

Introduction

Oxford Learner's Pocket Phrasal Verbs and Idioms can help you to increase your knowledge and understanding of this important aspect of vocabulary in one compact, easy-to-use book.

There are 134 two-page units, divided into 24 modules, with most modules covering different areas of an important topic, e.g. 'Family and friends' or 'Work'. There are also a number of units which provide important information about particular aspects of phrasal verbs such as grammar, style, or meanings of specific particles (e.g. *back*, *on* or *through*).

Each unit in a module presents and explains approximately 15 items of vocabulary. Some are presented through pictures, e.g. 'Physical actions' or 'Using phones and mobiles', but more often the vocabulary is presented in different types of text so that you can see the new phrasal verbs and idioms being used naturally. All the new vocabulary is shown in **bold** print.

After each text, a glossary explains the new vocabulary, and gives further important information to help you. This may be about grammar:

> take sb in OFTEN PASSIVE make sb believe sth that is not true. SYN deceive sb.

There is also information about style:

pack sth in INF stop doing an activity or a job.

There are synonyms or opposites, or related words from the same word family:

slow down go more slowly. OPP speed up.

stand-in sb who takes another person's place for a short period of time, especially to do their job. stand in (for sb) v.

There are common word partners:

put sth up build sth: *put up a building/ shelves/a fence.*

More information about a word or group of words is often included in a word focus:

WORD FOCUS

If you **ask for sth**, you speak or write to somebody because you want them to do something (see text).
If you **ask after sb**, you want news about them: *Michael was asking after you.*
If you **ask around**, you ask different people for information: *I don't know who can do the job, but I'll ask around.*

A word list is available on the website at www.oup.com/elt/wordskills which includes all the phrasal verbs and idioms explained in this book. You can use it as a reference for studying, or to test yourself.

This book can be used alongside many English courses. It includes most of the topics commonly found in course books, but teaches a range of phrasal verbs and idioms that course books do not have space for. There are more than 1,500 phrasal verbs and idioms taught in the book, corresponding to CEF levels B1-C2, with a particular emphasis on the higher levels C1-C2. This makes it ideal for learners who are preparing for exams such as IELTS and *Cambridge English: Proficiency* and *Advanced.*

What are phrasal verbs?

A phrasal verb consists of a base verb, e.g. *catch* or *look*, and one or two particles (adverb or preposition), e.g. *on* or *to.*

1 base verb 2 particle

I'll be late tonight, so don't ***wait up for*** *me.*

3 particle

This new computer game could ***catch on****.*
Paula was so angry she ***tore up*** *my letter.*

Sometimes the meaning of the phrasal verb is similar to the base verb.
I'm ***staying in*** *tonight.*
Sometimes the meaning is different.
You need to ***keep in with*** *the manager.*

You also need to know whether you can separate the verb and particle. (See 1.2.)

Separable
He failed the test but tried to ***laugh*** *it* ***off****.*

Not separable
They ***laughed at*** *me because of my clothes.*

One feature of phrasal verbs is that many of them have more than one meaning. (See 1.3.)

1 *We're* ***putting on*** *a concert next month.*
2 *Lucy is* ***putting on*** *her make-up.*
3 *Bernie sometimes* ***puts on*** *an accent.*

Most phrasal verbs are either neutral or informal in style. (See 1.4.)
Calm down*! You know Martin only says these things to* ***wind*** *you* ***up*** ▼.

wait up for sb not go to sleep until sb comes home.
catch on become popular or fashionable.
tear sth up destroy sth such as a piece of paper or cloth by pulling it into small pieces.
stay in stay at home.
keep in with sb stay friendly with sb, especially sb who can help you.
laugh sth off joke about sth in order to make people think you do not believe it to be serious or important.
laugh at sb say unkind things about sb that are intended to make them look stupid.
put sth on **1** organize an event, show, performance, etc.
2 spread a cream, liquid or other substance on your body or hair to protect it or make it look more attractive: *put on make-up.*
3 pretend to have a particular way of speaking or behaving.
calm down used to tell sb to be more relaxed and less emotional.

WORD FOCUS

Wind sb up is informal, and means to say something that will annoy or worry somebody, usually as a joke (see text). **Wind sth up**, however, is not informal. It can mean to close a company completely, or to bring something such as a speech or meeting to an end: *We'll have to wind up the meeting now.*

Grammar of phrasal verbs

There are three main types of phrasal verb:

1 Phrasal verbs with no object (intransitive).
I promised to help; I can't ***back out*** *now.*
How did the change in policy ***come about****?*
This pain just won't ***go away.***

2 Phrasal verbs which take an object (transitive) and are separable.
I think the dog ***frightened*** *him* ***away****.*
You may have to ***spell out*** *the reasons, otherwise the students won't understand.*
I said I'd ***bring*** *her book* ***back*** *tomorrow.*

With these verbs, you can usually put the object before or after the particle.
I ***put*** <u>*your name*</u> ***down.***
I ***put down*** <u>*your name*</u>*.*

If the object is a long phrase, it usually comes after the particle.
I ***put down*** <u>*everything they asked for*</u>*.*

If the object is a pronoun, it must come between the particle and the verb.
I ***put*** *it* ***down****. (I ~~put down it~~.)*

3 Phrasal verbs which take an object but cannot be separated by the object. These verbs may have one or two particles.
I haven't ***heard from*** *my cousin recently.*
(I haven't ~~heard my cousin from~~ recently.)
We haven't ***settled on*** *a name yet.*
They all ***went along with*** *the idea.*

back out decide not to do sth that you agreed to do.
come about happen, especially by chance.
go away disappear or stop existing.
frighten sb/sth away make a person or animal so afraid that they run away.
spell sth out (to sb) INF say or explain sth to sb very clearly to make sure that they understand it.
bring sth/sb back return sth/sb.
put sth down write sth on a piece of paper.
hear from sb if you have heard from sb, they have written to you, phoned you, emailed you, etc.
settle on sth if you settle on sth, you choose or make a decision about sth after thinking about it.
go along with sb/sth agree with a plan or decision that sb has made.

WORD FOCUS

The grammar of a phrasal verb is shown in this book by the way it is entered:
go away (type 1)
put sth down (type 2)
settle on sth/sb (type 3)
If you see brackets, e.g. **get through (sth)** or **help (sb) out**, it means that the verb can be used with or without an object:
I'll help her out. / I'll help out.
Objects are shown in this way:
spell sth out = the object (sth) is a thing.
help sb out = the object (sb) is a person.
go along with sb/sth = the object (sb/sth) can be a person or thing.

Multiple meaning

Many phrasal verbs have more than one meaning. Sometimes there is a connection between the different meanings. In these examples, the connection is the sense of appearing or becoming visible.

1 *My book* ***comes out*** *next month.*
2 *It's lovely when the sun* ***comes out.***
3 *The facts will* ***come out*** *soon.*

Sometimes there is no direct connection between the different meanings.

1 *Shall we* ***go out*** *tonight?*
2 *The fire has* ***gone out.***
3 *The show* ***goes out*** *tomorrow evening.*

Some phrasal verbs are transitive with one meaning and intransitive with another.
I can't hear the TV. Could you ***turn*** *it* ***up****?*
They didn't ***turn up*** *until nine o'clock.*

A second particle creates a new meaning.
The subject just ***came up*** *the other day.*
His work didn't ***come up to*** *standard.*
We ***came up against*** *all sorts of problems.*

Some phrasal verbs have many meanings.

1 *I can't* ***get into*** *these jeans.*
2 *Jason* ***got into*** *an argument with someone.*
3 *I've* ***got into*** *the habit of waking up early.*
4 *I'm really* ***getting into*** ▼ *Bollywood films.*

come out **1** be published.
2 if the sun comes out, it appears.
3 become known.

go out **1** leave the house and go somewhere, especially to do sth enjoyable.
2 if a fire or light goes out, it stops burning or shining.
3 if a programme goes out, it is shown on TV.

turn sth up increase the volume of sth. OPP turn sth down.

turn up (of a person) arrive.

come up be mentioned or discussed.

come up to sth reach a level that is good enough: *come up to standard.*

come up against sth/sb be faced with problems or be opposed by sb.

get into sth **1** INF put on a piece of clothing, especially with difficulty.
2 start or become involved in sth such as a conversation, a fight, an argument, etc.
3 develop a particular habit or routine: *get into the habit of doing sth.*
4 INF become interested in sth.

WORD FOCUS

In addition to the meanings above, **get into sth** has at least two more meanings.
5 (of a train, bus, etc.) arrive at a place: *When does the plane get into Rome?*
6 be accepted at a school or university, or chosen to play in a team: *I'm hoping to get into university next year.*

Style and register

Many phrasal verbs are neutral in style (not formal or informal), and they can be used in a wide range of situations.

*Let's **spread out** and search the whole area.*
*The neighbours **turned down** our invitation.*
*The students **put forward** some good ideas.*

However, phrasal verbs are most commonly used in spoken English and informal written English. In more formal spoken or written English, there is often a single word equivalent that we use instead.

Please extinguish all cigarettes now.
*'Can you **put** your cigarette **out** ▼, please?'*
They want to abolish the monarchy.
*'They want to **do away with** the monarchy.'*

Phrasal verbs that are particularly informal and used especially in spoken English are marked INF in this book. (See 22.7.)

*Who **dreamt up** this silly idea?*
*The reforms will **kick in** soon.*
*Barry said he was coming, then **cried off** at the last minute.*

A small number of phrasal verbs are more formal, and are marked FML. (See 22.8.)

*The government has **entered into** an agreement with private hospitals.*
*They refused to **enlarge upon** their plans.*

spread out if people in a group spread out, they move away from each other to cover a larger area.

turn sth down reject or refuse an offer, request or invitation.

put sth forward offer an idea, opinion, etc., especially so that people can discuss it and make a decision.

do away with sth INF bring sth to an end or get rid of sth. SYN abolish sth.

dream sth up INF have an idea, especially a very unusual or silly one.

kick in INF begin to have an effect.

cry off INF say that you cannot do sth that you promised or agreed to do.

enter into sth FML begin a discussion or start a formal arrangement: *enter into an agreement/a contract.*

enlarge on/upon sth FML say or write more about sth that has already been mentioned.

WORD FOCUS

If you **put out** a fire or cigarette, you stop it burning (see text). SYN **extinguish sth**.

If you **put yourself out (for sb)**, you make a special effort to do something for somebody: *I'm not putting myself out for Donnie; he's so lazy.*

Although these phrasal verbs look similar, the second one has a different meaning and is also more informal in style.

Nouns from phrasal verbs

We create nouns from some phrasal verbs.
*I thought the concert was a bit of a **letdown**.*
*We've got two doctors **on standby** ▼.*

These nouns do not always have a related phrasal verb, or one with the same meaning.
*There was a two-week **stand-off** in the talks.*
*There has been a big **breakthrough** in the treatment of diabetes.*

Many phrasal nouns are written as one word, e.g. *letdown*, but nouns with *-up*, *-in*, and *-off* are usually written with a hyphen.
*The film got a good **write-up** in the paper.*
*Mrs Gregory will be my **stand-in**.*
*He had a crash, and the car's a **write-off**.*

The plural is usually formed by adding *-s* to the particle.
*Did the teacher give you any **handouts**?*

Some phrasal verbs form nouns where the particle is at the beginning. These nouns are written as one word, and the plural form comes at the end of the word.
*The **upkeep** of the palace is enormous.*
*The company values your **input**.*
*When I got to the accident, there were quite a large number of **bystanders** ▼.*

letdown sth that makes you feel disappointed because it is not as good as you expected it to be. let sb down v.

stand-off (between A and B) a situation in which no agreement can be reached.

breakthrough a discovery or achievement that comes after a lot of hard work.

write-up an article in a paper or magazine in which sb gives their opinion of a new book, film, product, etc.

stand-in sb who takes another person's place, especially at work, for a short period of time. stand in (for sb) v.

write-off a vehicle that has been so badly damaged in an accident that it is not worth repairing it. write sth off v.

handout a piece of paper with information, exercises, etc. on it that is given to everyone in a group. hand sth out v.

upkeep the process and cost of keeping sth in good condition. keep sth up v.

input a person's contribution in the form of ideas, information, etc. which help in a process or to make a decision.

WORD FOCUS

Two nouns may be created from different meanings of the same phrasal verb, e.g. **stand by**. If you are **on standby**, you are available to help if needed in a particular situation. A **bystander** is someone who watches what is happening, e.g. an accident, but is not directly involved.

Adjectives from phrasal verbs

A number of adjectives are formed from related phrasal verbs.

There are still ***ongoing*** *discussions.*
The FA Cup is a ***knockout*** *competition.*
Clive's proposal was just a ***watered-down*** *version of the original plan.*
She made some very ***outspoken*** *remarks.*
The bedroom has two ***built-in*** *wardrobes.*

The same adjective may correspond with different meanings of the related verb.

1 *The fish was tasty, but the smell was a bit* ***off-putting*** ▼.
2 *The noise was very* ***off-putting*** ▼.
1 *The children were* ***worn out*** *after the long walk.*
2 *My trainers are pretty* ***worn out***.

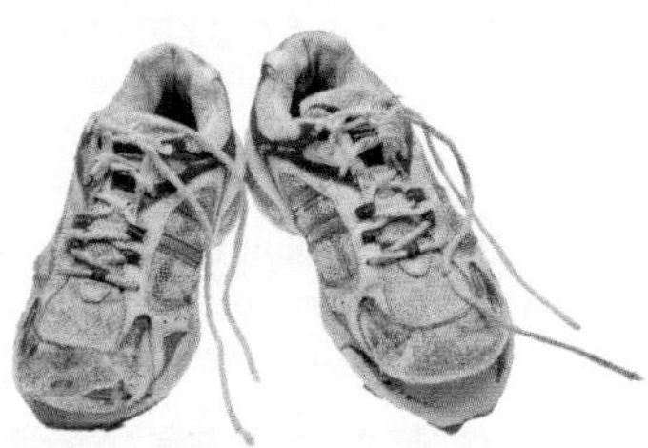

A phrasal adjective usually has a very similar meaning to the related phrasal verb, but sometimes the meaning changes slightly.

I'm looking for a more ***go-ahead*** *company.*
We can ***go ahead*** *with the new development.*

ongoing continuing to happen or develop. go on v.

knockout in a knockout competition, only the winning team or players at each stage continue to play in the competition. knock sb out v.

watered-down a watered-down idea, plan, statement, etc. has been made less powerful, detailed, offensive, etc. than it was originally. water sth down v.

outspoken expressing what sb thinks, even if it shocks or upsets people. speak out (against sth/sb) v.

built-in constructed as part of sth and not separated from it. build sth in v.

worn out **1** if sb is worn out, they feel very tired, especially after hard work or exercise. wear sb out v. **2** if sth is worn out, it is damaged, or no longer useful, because it has been used a lot. wear sth out v.

go-ahead happy to try new ideas, methods, etc. and therefore more likely to succeed.

go ahead start or continue to do sth, especially after getting permission.

WORD FOCUS

Off-putting can describe somebody or something that is unpleasant (see example 1). **put sb off sb/sth** v. It can also be used to describe somebody or something that disturbs or distracts you so that you find it difficult to concentrate (see example 2). **put sb off** v.

What are idioms?

Idioms are expressions whose meaning is often difficult to understand by looking at the individual words. Seeing idioms in context can sometimes make them clearer.

She ***has a thing about*** *men with beards.*
My parents arrived ***out of the blue*** *today.*
These shoes will be fine ***for the time being.***
I'm afraid I ***put my foot in it.***

Some idioms are easier to understand, but are still called idioms because they are fixed expressions which need to be learnt as whole phrases.

After the break-up, things ***went from bad to worse.***
I know enough Spanish to ***make myself understood.***

With some idioms there is a choice of words without changing the meaning.

Are you going? ~ ***It/That depends.***
He arrived ***at the last minute/moment.*** ▼

Idioms can be formed from such everyday words that you may not notice them or realize they are idioms.

I ***didn't think much of*** *the film.*
Karen ***is nothing like*** *her sister.*
I'm enjoying my new job ***so far.***
The room was ***lovely and warm.***

have a thing about sth/sb INF have a strong liking for or dislike of sth/sb.

out of the blue INF suddenly and unexpectedly.

for the time being for now and the immediate future.

put your foot in it INF accidentally say sth that embarrasses, upsets or annoys sb.

go from bad to worse (of a bad situation) become even worse.

make yourself understood make your meaning clear, especially in another language.

it/that depends used when you cannot give a definite answer because different things are possible in the situation.

not think much of sth/sb not like sth/sb very much.

be nothing like sb/sth not be similar to sb or sth in any way.

so far until now.

lovely and warm, cool, soft, etc. used to emphasize the pleasant quality that sth has: *The bed was lovely and soft.*

WORD FOCUS

If you arrive **at the last minute/moment**, you arrive at the latest possible time before an event; you are almost late. We use **minute** in several other idioms.

any minute very soon: *They'll be here any minute.*

the minute as soon as: *I want to see him the minute he gets here.*

Physical actions

He's **fallen over**.

She's **tripped over** the log.

The cyclist has **knocked** him **over/down**.

She's **bumped into** the lamppost.

She's **lying down**.

He's **getting up**.

He's **bending down/over**.

He's **turning round/around** to talk to his friend.

A healthy eating plan

BRAD: I realized I'd **put on** weight when my trousers started to feel a bit tight. But when I couldn't **do up** the jacket on my best suit, I knew right away it was time to **turn over a new leaf** – **as far as** food **was concerned**, anyway. I mentioned this to a friend, who sent me details of an internet dieting programme. I thought it was worth trying, so I **signed up for** it.

The website sent me weekly recipes of healthy diet meals, but also recommended that I should **cut down on** the actual portion size, and obviously **cut out** junk food, sweets, fizzy drinks, etc. It was **hard going** at first because it meant changing a number of habits, but I **kept to** the diet very rigidly and after a while, the weight started to **fall off**. I combined it with **working out** at the gym, but I know the diet was the main thing that helped.

A normal meal now **fills me up**, so I'm not constantly looking for extra snacks (which are my big temptation). I'm going away on holiday next week, happy to **show off** ▼ my new image! I'm glad I **faced up to** my problem. •

put on (weight) become heavier.

do sth up fasten an item of clothing which has buttons or a zip.

turn over a new leaf start to act or behave in a better way.

as far as sth/sb is concerned used to say which person or thing you are talking about.

sign up (for sth) arrange to do a course, join a group, etc. by adding your name to a list of people doing it.

cut down (on sth) eat, drink or use less of sth.

cut sth out stop eating or drinking sth, especially sth that is bad for you.

hard going needing a lot of effort.

keep to sth follow a rule or an agreement, by doing what you said you would do.

fall off decrease in quantity or quality.

work out make your body fit and strong by doing a programme of regular exercises. workout N.

fill sb up (of food) make sb feel completely full.

face up to sth accept and deal with sth that is difficult or unpleasant.

WORD FOCUS

If you **show sth off**, you show people something that you are proud of. If you **show off**, INF, DISAPPROVING, you try to impress people by talking about your abilities, possessions or achievements (see also 16.4).

Common ailments

Li: Hi, Rose! How are things?

Rose: I'm feeling a bit **under the weather**, actually. I had some shellfish round at my sister's last night, and it **didn't agree with** me.

Li: Oh, dear! Were you sick?

Rose: Yes, I was **throwing up** all night.

Li: Well, just drink water and eat dry toast – that's what Mum recommends.

Rose: I will – when I can **keep** something **down**!

Ali: I hear Jamie's **picked up** a bug.

Ann: Yes, there are lots of them **going round** at the moment. I don't think it's serious, but he's looking pretty **washed out** ▼, so I'm keeping him at home today.

Ali: Well, **it won't do him any harm** to **take it easy** for **a day or two**.

Ann: No, these things can **take it out of** you, but I'm sure he'll **get over** it soon.

Ali: Yeah, he's young – he'll be **on the mend** in no time!

Joc: Dad's been **complaining of** a bad back again.

Lottie: Yes, it usually **flares up** when he's been gardening.

under the weather INF feeling slightly sick or not as well as usual.

not agree with sb (of food) make you feel sick or ill.

throw up INF bring food from your stomach back out through your mouth.

keep sth down succeed in keeping food in your stomach even if you feel sick.

pick sth up catch an infectious illness.

go round if an illness is going round, people are catching it from each other.

it won't/wouldn't do (sb) any harm used to say what you think sb should do.

take it/things easy relax and avoid doing too much or working too hard. SYN put your feet up.

a day or two one or a few days.

take it/a lot out of sb INF make sb feel mentally or physically tired.

get over sth start to feel better or well again after an illness or sth unpleasant.

on the mend getting better after an illness or injury.

complain of sth say that you are suffering from sth, e.g. pain, an illness.

flare up suddenly start again or become worse.

WORD FOCUS

If you look **washed out** INF, you look pale, ill or tired. If you are **worn out** or **wiped out** INF, you are extremely tired.

Going to hospital

EVA: When I was eight, I was **knocked over** by a bike outside my house. Of course, I **burst into tears** – it was mainly the shock, but I'd cut my knee badly and my arm was starting to swell. People **crowded round**, trying to help. Fortunately a doctor was **passing by** and he sent me to hospital to get **checked over**. When I got there, the nurse **calmed me down**, and they cleaned and **stitched up** the cut. Back at home, Mum **took care of** me and gave me ice cream. After a day or two, the pain **eased off** and the swelling **went down**. They **took** the stitches **out** a week later.

FRANCISCO: Not long ago, I had to go to hospital to **have** my wisdom teeth **out**. I hate injections **at the best of times**, but on this occasion, when they tried to give me an anaesthetic, I just **passed out** ▼. I felt stupid when I **came to** ▼!

knock sb over/down hit sb with a vehicle so that they fall and are injured or killed.
burst into tears start crying suddenly.
crowd round/around (sb/sth) gather in large numbers around sb/sth.
pass by (sth/sb) go past. A person who goes past is a passer-by N.
check sb/sth over examine sb/sth to see if there is anything wrong with them/it.
calm sb down make sb feel more relaxed and less anxious or emotional.
stitch sb/sth up join sb's skin together after it has been cut.
take care of sb do the necessary things for sb who needs help. SYN look after sb.
ease off if sth unpleasant, e.g. pain, eases off, it gets better or becomes less.
go down (of swelling) become less.
take sth out remove sth from sb's body.
have sth out have a tooth removed from your mouth, or an organ, e.g. an appendix, removed from your body.
at the best of times used to say that sth is difficult or unpleasant, even when the circumstances are good.

WORD FOCUS

When some people see blood, they may **pass out** (= lose consciousness) SYN **black out.** After a minute or two, they **come to** SYN **come round** (= become conscious again).

Health headlines

SMOKERS ENCOURAGED TO **TAKE UP** SMOKELESS NICOTINE CIGARETTES

Nurses urged to **guard against** becoming too emotionally attached to patients

England Captain **on verge of breakdown**

JAZZ LEGEND **PASSES AWAY** IN HIS SLEEP

RACING DRIVER **PULLS THROUGH** OPERATION

Discovery **leads to** new anti-stress drug

Asthma symptoms **brought on by** cat allergy

FILM STAR **CHECKS INTO** CLINIC

SMOKING-RELATED DISEASES **ON THE RISE**

Workers **deprived of** sleep cost industry billions

HOSPITAL JOBS **SHAKE-UP** PUTS EMERGENCY PATIENTS **AT RISK**

DOCTORS WARNED TO **BE ON THEIR GUARD** FOR TUBERCULOSIS

Police **search out** gang members who attacked boy

take sth up start doing sth regularly as a habit, job or interest.
guard against sth take care to prevent sth or protect yourself from sth.
on the verge of sth very near to the moment when sth happens.
breakdown a period of mental illness in which sb becomes very depressed and anxious and cannot deal with normal life.
pass away die. Pass away is often used in place of 'die' to avoid upsetting sb.
pull through (sth) manage to stay alive after a serious illness, an injury or an operation.
lead to sth have a particular result or outcome. SYN result in sth.
bring sth on make sth develop or happen, especially sth unpleasant.
check into sth arrive at a hospital or hotel and begin your stay there.
on the rise increasing. SYN on the increase.
deprive sb of sth prevent sb from having or doing sth, especially sth important.
be on (your) guard be very careful and prepared for sth dangerous or difficult.
shake-up a situation in which changes are made to a company, organization, etc. to improve the way it works.
at risk in danger of sth unpleasant or harmful happening: *put sb/sth at risk.*
search sth/sb out look for sb/sth until you find them. SYN track sb/sth down.

Feelings

How are you feeling today?

ANNIE I was a bit **down in the dumps** this morning for various reasons, but a friend gave me a big bunch of flowers which **brought a smile to my face** ▼.

LEO I watched my little girl sing a song at a school concert today. I was **choking back** the tears; I was just so proud of her.

FINN My brother **started on at** me **about** my driving, and that made me **tense up**. I'm always **on edge** when he's in the passenger seat, because he's so critical.

RONI **I'm** a bit **shaken up**. I went to look out of the window and a strange man was right there, staring at me. I nearly **jumped out of my skin**, but fortunately he ran off. I was **shaking like a leaf** afterwards.

EVIE My boyfriend rang me from the States this morning. It really **made** my **day**.

ROB I went to the gym, and that really **tired** me **out**. But then I had a coffee and **a sit-down**, and I **perked up** a bit.

JOSH I tend to **bottle up** my feelings, but today I **got** really **worked up** because of a horrible text from my boss. It was stupid, but I had to go for a walk to **cool down**.

MIA I've been **on tenterhooks** all day, waiting for my exam results!

down in the dumps INF feeling unhappy.
choke sth back manage with difficulty to control your tears, feelings, etc.
start on at sb (about sth) INF criticize sb or start to complain about sth.
tense up if you tense up, your muscles become tight or stiff.
on edge nervous because you are expecting sth bad to happen.
shake sb up give sb a very unpleasant shock so that they are upset or frightened.
jump out of your skin INF move suddenly because you are surprised or afraid.
shake like a leaf make sudden, quick movements, up and down or side to side, because you are frightened or nervous.
make sb's day make sb feel very happy.
tire sb out make sb feel very tired.
a sit-down a rest while sitting in a chair.
perk up INF feel more cheerful or lively after feeling sad, ill, etc. (Also perk sb up.)
bottle sth up hide your feelings, especially over a long period of time.
be/get worked up INF be/get very upset or excited about sth.
cool down become less angry or excited.
on tenterhooks nervous because you do not know what is going to happen.

WORD FOCUS

If something **brings a smile to your face**, it makes you happy. If something **brings tears to your eyes**, it makes you cry, or feel as if you are going to cry.

Growing up

I was born in London, but we **moved away** when I was four to be closer to my grandparents, and I **grew up** in a medium-sized town in the north of England. My dad was always **on the road** with his job, so I **was** mainly **brought up** ▼ by my mother and grandparents.

As a child I **looked forward to** Saturdays. Grandad took me to watch Chesterfield, my local football team. I loved it, and he **got** quite **carried away** watching football; it was the only time I ever heard him swear. Sundays, however, were boring. My parents wouldn't **let** me **out** to play in the street: I had to **stay in** and sometimes **give** my mother **a hand** with the housework. I could **invite** friends **round**, but that was only because my mother wanted to **keep an eye on** me.

Dad occasionally **took** us **out** to the cinema or for a picnic, which was good fun. And in the summer we always **went away** for two weeks, often to strange places in Scotland I'd never **heard of.** ■

move away stop living in one place and go to live in another.
grow up change from being a baby or child into an older child or adult. A grown-up is an adult.
on the road travelling, often because of a job.
look forward to sth feel happy and excited about sth that is going to happen.
get/be carried away become so excited that you lose control of your feelings.
let sb/sth out allow a person or an animal to leave a room, house, etc.
stay in remain in your home for a period of time.
give sb a hand help sb to do sth.
invite sb round/over ask sb to come to your house, for example for a meal.
keep an eye on sb watch sb and look after them so that they cannot be harmed.
take sb out go to a club, restaurant, etc. with sb that you have invited.
go away leave home for a period of time, especially to go on holiday.
hear of sth if you have heard of sth, you know about it because you have read or been told about it.

WORD FOCUS

If you **bring** a child **up**, you look after them until they become an adult. This verb is often passive. **upbringing** N.
I had a very different upbringing from my wife.

What makes a good parent?

Being a good parent is not easy, and all parents make mistakes. But here are some things to bear in mind.

Good parents:

- shouldn't have favourites or **pick on** one child more than another.
- shouldn't **take sides** ▼ when children argue with one another.
- shouldn't **take** it **out on** their children when they (the parents) are in a bad mood.
- should have their arguments **in private**, not in front of their children.
- should **look on** each child **as** an individual.
- should give them unconditional love, but also be prepared to **lay down the law** when necessary, e.g. at bedtimes.
- should learn to **turn a blind eye to** small, unimportant things that children do wrong.
- should talk and listen to their children, and if necessary, be **a shoulder to cry on**.
- should **seek out** interesting things to do in the neighbourhood.
- should welcome their children's friends and **get to know** them.
- should try to establish routines for their children. Kids **thrive on** routines and knowing what their day will be like.
- should make friends with parents who have children the same age, so they can **talk through** issues that affect them all.

bear sth in mind remember or consider sth. (Also bear in mind that … .)
pick on sb keep treating sb badly or unfairly, especially by criticizing them.
take sth out on sb make sb suffer because you are angry, upset or tired, even though it is not their fault.
in private in a place or situation where other people cannot watch or listen. OPP in public.
look on sb as sb/sth think about sb in a particular way.
lay down the law tell sb firmly what they should or should not do.
turn a blind eye (to sth) pretend not to notice sth bad happening, because you do not want to do anything about it.
a shoulder to cry on sb who listens to you with sympathy when you have problems.
seek sb/sth out find sb or sth by looking in a determined way.
get to know sb start to be familiar with sb and become friends.
thrive on sth become successful or happy in a situation.
talk sth through discuss sth carefully until you are sure you understand it.

WORD FOCUS

If you **take sides** in a disagreement, you show support for one person and not others. If you **are on sb's side**, you support and agree with them.

Mother and daughter

WHEN Deborah Tannen started writing her book about mother/daughter relationships, she wanted to know why she didn't **get on** better **with** her own mother.

'Yes, I adored her,' she says, 'but she also **drove** me **mad**.' Perhaps this **stems from** the fact that the mother/daughter relationship is such a great source of both love and anger. For example, you tell your mother you bought a handbag and she shares your excitement. Then you tell her you're on a diet and she says, 'but will you **keep** it **up**?'. It's probably a harmless remark, but for someone who **knows** you **inside out** and **is supposed to be** on your side, why does she sometimes **insist on** ▼ making you feel a failure?

What is **at issue** here is the fact that mothers and daughters are reflections of each other (in a way that mothers and sons obviously aren't), and that forces them to **face up to** who they are and what they want to be. And mothers, of course, are always looking to see whether their daughter **turns out** like them.

Another thing is that women love to talk. It is the glue that **holds** a relationship **together**, but can also **tear** it **apart**. It is often said that women talk to each other whereas men do things with each other. •

get on (with sb) have a good relationship (with sb).
drive sb mad INF make sb very angry. SYN drive sb round the bend INF.
stem from sth be caused by sth.
keep sth up keep doing sth, or maintain sth at the same level or standard.
know sb/sth inside out know sb/sth very well. (Also know sth like the back of your hand.)
be supposed to be/do sth be expected to behave in a particular way, especially according to a custom, rule or arrangement.
at issue if sth is at issue, it is an important aspect of a situation or subject under discussion.
face up to sth accept and deal with sth that is difficult or unpleasant.
turn out develop in a particular way or have a particular result.
hold sth/sb together keep sth or two or more people united and strong.
tear sth apart damage or destroy sth such as a relationship. SYN tear sth to pieces/shreds.

WORD FOCUS

Insist on sth has different meanings.
1 continue doing something even if it is annoying or strange (see text).
2 say firmly that you want something or that something must happen: *He insisted on an answer. She insisted on paying for the meal.*

What makes a good friend?

'**To my mind**, a good friend is someone you can **count on** ▼, and someone who will **stand by** you **when the going gets tough**.'

'My best friend is the one who **brings out the best in** me. ' *Henry Ford*

'Alex is my best friend; he's **a great laugh**. When I'm down he **cheers** me **up**.'

'A friend is someone who will **put up with** your faults because they like you.'

'I **get by** with a little help from my friends.' *Lennon and McCartney*

'A good friend is somebody who is there when you need them: someone who'll **get behind** you and won't **let** you **down**.'

'I think a good friend is someone you **relate to** – someone who shares your interests and sense of humour.'

'The better part of one's life **consists of** friendships.' *Abraham Lincoln*

'For me, a good friend is anyone who **livens up** the party!'

to my mind used to emphasize that you are expressing your own opinion.

stand by sb help and support sb, especially when they are having problems.

when the going gets tough INF in difficult situations.

bring out the best/worst in sb make sb behave in the best or worst way possible.

a (good/great) laugh someone who is fun to be with.

cheer sb up make sb feel happier or less sad.

put up with sth/sb accept sth/sb unpleasant in a patient way; tolerate sth/sb.

get by manage to live or survive with sth, or with what you have.

get behind sb support sb or help them in what they are trying to do.

let sb down not help or support sb in the way that they are hoping and expecting.

relate to sb be able to understand the way that sb feels and thinks.

consist of sth be formed from the things or people mentioned.

liven sth up make sth more interesting or exciting.

WORD FOCUS

If you can **count on sb**, you can trust them, or trust them to do something for you. You can also use **rely on sb** or **depend on sb** in this context.

Friendships at work

Danger: friends at work

WHEN SIOBHAN MOORE started her first job, she **made friends with** a colleague called Tricia. They started going out after work, and one night, Siobhan **happened to** mention that she liked their head of department, and she thought he liked her too. Tricia immediately tried to **get** more details **out of** her, and Siobhan went home worrying whether Tricia would **keep** the conversation **to herself**. Fortunately, the romance **came to nothing** and the friendship survived. But it was a warning.

Friendships at work can be a problem, and it's hard to know where to **draw the line**. According to sociologist Dr Jan Yager, the trick is not to **confide in** colleagues. "**Steer clear of** personal information or strong opinions if possible."

Claire Langman had a friend at work, and they **got along** very well until the two of them **went for** ▼ the same promotion. "I then realized I was trying to persuade others to **find fault with** my competitor," says Claire. "I wasn't proud of that."

Friendships can also **mess up** the dynamics of an office because two people who become friends can appear a stronger unit and that creates an imbalance.

make friends (with sb) become friends (with sb).

happen to do sth do sth by chance.

get sth out of sb persuade sb to give you more information about sth.

keep sth to yourself not tell other people about sth. (If you keep yourself to yourself, you stay alone, rather than spending time with other people.)

come to nothing if sth comes to nothing, it is not successful and goes no further.

draw the line (at sth) set a limit where you say that you will no longer allow or accept sth.

confide in sb tell sb personal information because you feel that you can trust them.

steer clear of sth/sb avoid sth/sb because it may be dangerous or cause you problems.

get along (of two or more people) like each other and have a good relationship.

find fault with sb criticize sb, often after trying to find mistakes they have made.

mess sth up damage or spoil sth.

WORD FOCUS

Go for sth/sb INF has different meanings.
1 try to get something, e.g. a job, that you have to compete for (see text).
2 like a particular kind of person or thing: *What type of men do you go for?*
3 choose a particular kind of thing: *I'm going for the fish. What about you?*

Starting a new relationship

Are you looking for a new partner? You may have **ended up** with the wrong one last time, but there are still wonderful people **out there**. However, it is important that you've **got over** ▼ any previous relationships and feel you are now ready to start a new relationship.

When you **go out with** someone, don't expect too much on the first date, but if you have a good time, **there's no harm in** texting or phoning to say you enjoyed it. Don't **insist on** another date but try a gentle, 'would you like to **meet up** again?' Even if the first date wasn't a great success – remember both parties may have been very nervous – **give it a** second **try**. Then, if it doesn't **work out**, you can **cut your losses** and **move on**.

If things go well, consider how well he or she **fits in with** your friends, and whether you feel **at ease** with their friends. And don't forget your own friends; you need to spend time with them too.

Most important of all, listen to your **gut feeling** – it's rarely wrong.

end up find yourself in a particular situation or place that you did not plan to be in.
out there in society, or in the world.
go out with sb have a romantic meeting or relationship with sb.
there's no harm in doing sth used to say that doing sth will not cause problems and may help a situation.
insist on sth say firmly that you want sth or that sth must happen.
meet up INF (of two or more people) meet by arrangement. (Also meet up with sb.)
give sth a try do sth to find out what happens, or to find out whether sth is good, effective, etc.
work out develop in a successful way.
cut your losses get out of a bad situation before it gets worse instead of waiting to see if it improves.
move on start doing sth new.
fit in with sb/sth live, work, etc. in an easy and natural way with sb/sth.
at ease confident and relaxed.
gut feeling a feeling that you are certain is right, although you cannot explain why.

WORD FOCUS

If you **get over sth/sb**, you recover from the end of a relationship (see text), a difficult experience, an illness or shock: *It took me ages to get over my operation. She was disappointed about failing the exam, but she'll get over it.*

Ending a relationship

It's never easy to end a relationship, but if things are **going wrong**, it may be better to **break up** rather than allow a relationship to **drag on** for ages making both of you unhappy. Here is some advice to make the **break-up** less painful.

1. Make sure you **talk over** any problems you have first. Every relationship has its **ups and downs,** and with full and open discussion you may be able to **sort** things **out** between you.
2. If you finally decide that the relationship has **come to an end**, don't just **walk away** ▼. End it **in person**, not by phone, email or text message, and do it **in private.**
3. Break the news calmly, and don't **get into** an argument. Make sure you know why you want to split up and can explain your reasons clearly.
4. **Focus on** why the relationship is not working for you; don't spend your time blaming the other person.
5. Once you've **made up your mind, stick to** your decision. It may seem unkind, but it's better for both of you like that.
6. Don't **drag** the conversation **out**. Give yourself a clear reason why you have to stop at a certain point, and then leave.

go wrong develop badly and cause problems.

break up (of two people) end a romantic relationship. (Also break up with sb.) SYN split up (with sb). break-up N.

drag on continue for too long.

talk sth over (with sb) discuss a problem or plan.

ups and downs a mix of good times and bad times.

sort sth out do what is necessary to deal with a problem successfully.

come to an end finish.

in person if you do sth in person, you do it yourself, instead of writing, phoning or sending sb else to do it.

in private without other people being present. OPP in public.

get into sth start or become involved in sth such as a discussion, argument, fight, etc.

focus on sth concentrate on sth and pay particular attention to it.

make up your mind make a decision.

stick to sth continue to do sth even though it is difficult.

drag sth out make sth continue longer than is necessary.

WORD FOCUS

If you **walk away (from sb/sth)**, you leave a difficult relationship or situation instead of trying to deal with it. If you **walk out (on sb/sth)**, you suddenly leave a person or situation that needs you.

How did we meet?

CONRAD joined the company where I work last May. I remember his very first day – we were **queuing up** together at the staff coffee machine, and I suddenly realized he was trying to **chat** me **up**. This **took** me a bit **by surprise** because he was junior to me in the company and also three years younger. But he was very self-confident, in fact a bit too self-confident **for my liking**, so when he **asked** me **out** the following day, I made it very clear the answer was 'no'. But that didn't **put** him **off** at all. He **kept on** asking, and **in the end** I just **gave in**. I agreed to go to a friend's party with him, and actually we had a really nice time. He was quite different when we were **on our own**, and we started **going out together**; it's been three months now. We've **fallen out** a couple of times when he hasn't **shown up** for a date, or he's been late, but we always seem to **make up**, and we're still together. ■

queue (up) wait in a line of people to do sth, have sth, or go somewhere.

chat sb up INF start a conversation with sb because you are romantically attracted to them.

take sb by surprise do sth that is unexpected and may shock sb.

for my liking if you say that sb is too self-confident for your liking, you would like them to be less self-confident.

ask sb out invite sb to go somewhere with you, especially as a way of starting a romantic relationship with them.

put sb off make sb not want to do sth, or make sb not like sb/sth.

keep on doing sth do sth many times.

in the end finally; after a long period of time or series of events.

give in (to sb/sth) agree to do sth that perhaps you did not want to do.

on your own alone; not with other people.

go out together (of two people) spend time together in a romantic relationship. (Also go out with sb.)

fall out (of two people) have an argument or no longer be friends. (Also fall out with sb.)

show up INF arrive where you have arranged to meet sb.

make up (of two people) end a disagreement and become friends again. (Also make up with sb.)

Starting again

Second time lucky

CAROLINE: I was only just sixteen when I met Robbie. We went out together for two years and then all through university. At the time I felt sure we were going to be together for the rest of our lives. But when we left university and started our careers, things didn't **work out** ▼ and unfortunately, we began to **drift apart**. It all **came to a head** when Robbie was offered a job abroad: he decided to take it, but I wanted to **stay put** in England, and eventually we **split up**.

For two years after that I didn't have a real boyfriend, but I was always confident that something would **turn up**. And it did. I met Gavin at the local gym where he used to **work out** ▼. We **got together** and quickly realized that this was the relationship we had both been **looking for**. Our plan now is to **settle down** and get married; we're extremely happy.

In retrospect, I think that Robbie and I met too early. In a way, we both **missed out on** our youth – the time when you can just **let your hair down** and not think about marriage or settling down.

drift apart if two or more people drift apart, their relationship gradually ends.

come to a head if a problem or situation comes to a head, it suddenly becomes much worse and has to be dealt with.

stay put remain in one place or position.

split up (of two people) end a romantic relationship. (Also split up with sb.)

turn up if sth turns up, it happens unexpectedly or by chance.

get together INF start a romantic relationship.

look for sth hope to get sth that you want or need.

settle down begin to live a quieter life by getting married or staying permanently in the same place.

in retrospect thinking back to a time in the past, often with knowledge that you did not have then. SYN with hindsight.

miss out on sth if you miss out on sth, you lose an opportunity to do or have sth.

let your hair down INF relax and enjoy yourself, especially in a lively way and without having to worry about anything.

WORD FOCUS

Work out has different meanings.
1 be successful, or end in a particular way (see paragraph 1 in the text).
2 do physical exercise as a way of keeping fit (see paragraph 2).
workout N.

Ex-girlfriends

Robbie's love life

Emily was my first real girlfriend. We were together for two years, and I don't know how she **put up with** me. I was very immature and not very nice to her some of the time. When she finally **finished with** me, I asked her why it took her so long. She said she did**n't have the heart to** tell me that it was over.

Ruby and I met a couple of months later. I **fell for** her **in a big way**. In fact, after two weeks I told her I was in love with her. She just said I was being silly, but I still adored her. Then I found out that she was **cheating on** me. That was the end of that.

Megan and I **hit it off** immediately. She **reminded** me **of** Emily in lots of ways. I felt I could **confide in** her, and she always said that I **cheered** her **up**. We **got on** really well, but last month she said she wanted me to **move in with** her. I thought it was a good idea at first, but then I started to **get cold feet**. Last week I told her I wanted to end the relationship. •

put up with sb/sth accept sb/sth unpleasant in a patient way; tolerate sb/sth.

finish with sb end a romantic relationship with sb.

not have the heart to do sth not be able to do or say sth because you think it would make sb unhappy.

fall for sb be very attracted to sb and start to love them.

in a big way INF used to emphasize the degree that you do or feel sth.

cheat on sb be unfaithful to your husband, wife or partner by having a relationship with sb else.

hit it off INF if two people hit it off when they meet for the first time, they like each other.

remind sb of sb make sb think of sb else because of a likeness or similarity.

confide in sb tell sb secret or personal information because you trust them.

cheer sb up make sb happier or more cheerful.

get on if two people get on, they like each other and have a good relationship. (Also get on with sb.) SYN get along (with sb).

move in with sb start living with sb in the house or flat where they already live.

get/have cold feet start to feel nervous about sth you have planned or agreed to do.

Weather

People from overseas often say that British people **go on about** the weather, but there is a reason for it: British weather not only changes **from one day to the next** ▼, but sometimes from one hour to the next. The day can **start off** with fine weather – the sun **comes up** and there's a bright blue sky. Then, by nine o'clock it begins to **cloud over**, and by mid-morning it's **pouring down**. Ten minutes later, the rain **eases off**, the sun **comes out**, it starts to **brighten up**, and it's fine again. By mid-afternoon the wind might **pick up**, bringing with it more rain, but by the end of the day it's dry. Perhaps this is why the British often tell others to **make the most of** the good weather while it lasts.

You would think the British would be prepared for anything, yet they**'re** still **caught out** by the weather. More than ten centimetres of snow in the winter and transport **grinds to a halt**; more than a few weeks of hot weather in the summer and there are warnings of water shortages!

go on (and on) about sth talk so much about sth that people get bored.
start off begin in a particular way.
come up (of the sun) rise in the morning. OPP go down.
cloud over become cloudy.
pour (down) rain very hard. SYN pour with rain.
ease off become less strong, unpleasant, etc.
come out (of the sun) appear from behind clouds.
brighten up if the weather brightens up, it becomes sunnier.
pick up if the wind picks up, it becomes stronger.
make the most of sth enjoy sth while you have the opportunity.
catch sb out OFTEN PASSIVE surprise sb by putting them in a difficult situation that they are not prepared for.
grind to a halt if traffic grinds to a halt, it moves very slowly and then stops. SYN grind to a standstill.

WORD FOCUS

If a situation changes **from one day to the next**, it is uncertain and not likely to stay the same each day (see text).
If something changes **from day to day**, it often changes: *The weather can change from day to day.*
If something happens **day after day**, it happens repeatedly, and is usually annoying: *We had rain day after day.*

Food

What does food mean to you?

MARCIA When I'm not eating, I seem to be either cooking or buying food, so my life **revolves around** food.

KV I don't get these people who **live for** food. I usually just **heat up** something from a can, or **pick up** a **takeaway**.

ASHLEY I regularly **go on a diet**, so I really have to think about what I'm eating. I've already **given up** chocolate, and at the moment I'm trying to **cut down on** my carbohydrate intake. Most of the time, though, I'**m starving**.

JAY Food is important provided you eat the right things. I've **cut out** junk food altogether, and I'm now really careful about eating too much dairy as well. But **having said that**, I couldn't **go without** my chocolate!

SENSOR I eat and eat, but I'm still **thin as a rake**. I guess I just **burn off** the calories with all the exercise I get.

RHONDA For me food is a social thing. When I want to see friends, I **ask** them **over** for a meal, or we **eat out** somewhere.

revolve around sth/sb have sth/sb as the most important part.

live for sth consider sth to be the most important thing in your life.

heat sth up make sth that has been cooked before warm or hot. SYN warm sth up.

pick sth up INF buy sth, especially cheaply or by chance.

takeaway a meal that you buy in a restaurant or shop to eat at home. take sth away v.

go/be on a diet try to get thinner by eating a limited range of food.

give sth up stop doing or having sth.

cut down on sth reduce the size, amount or number of sth.

be starving INF be very hungry.

cut sth out stop eating sth or doing sth, especially because it is bad for your health.

having said that INF used to introduce an opinion that makes what you have just said seem less strong.

go without sth live without sth that you need or would like to have.

(as) thin as a rake very thin.

burn sth off reduce calories, weight, etc. by using energy through exercise.

ask sb over invite sb to come to your house, usually for a drink or a meal.

eat out eat in a restaurant. (eat in = eat at home.)

Cooking

Mushroom risotto

  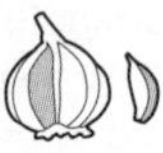

Preparation method

1 In a pan, fry the mushrooms gently and put **to one side. At the same time**, soak the dried porcini in a little warm water.

2 Gently fry the chopped onion and garlic. If you don't like garlic, **leave** it **out**.

3 Add the rice, then the white wine, and stir until the wine has almost evaporated. Now add the mushrooms and porcini.

4 Now you can add the hot chicken stock, **a bit at a time**, and stir fairly continuously until the rice has absorbed the stock. This will take about 15 minutes, but you should still be able to **clear up as you go along**.

5 **By the time** you've **used up** all the stock, the risotto should be tender. Take it off the heat, **stir in** some butter, half the parmesan and some parsley, and leave it to rest for a few minutes – this will **finish off** the risotto and make it especially creamy.

6 **Serve up** the risotto while hot and **hand round** the rest of the parmesan.

You can **heat up** any **leftovers** ▼ the next day, but in my experience, guests usually **polish** it all **off** at the table.

to/on one side in a place that is not directly in front of you or where you are working.

at the same time used to say that two or more things happen together.

leave sth/sb out not include sth or sb.

a bit at a time in small stages over a period of time.

clear (sth) up make a place clean and tidy.

as you go along if you do sth as you go along, you do it while you are doing sth else.

by the time used to say what has already happened at the time that sth else happens.

use sth up use all of sth so that there is none left.

stir sth in add sth to a liquid or other substance and mix it.

finish sth off do the last part of sth so that it is complete.

serve sth up put food onto plates and give it to people to eat.

hand sth around/round give sth to other people in a group.

heat sth up make sth that has been cooked before warm or hot. SYN warm sth up.

polish sth off INF finish sth, especially food, very quickly.

WORD FOCUS

Leftovers PL N refers to food that remains after you have eaten. The verb form is **be left over (from sth)**: *There is still some chicken left over from yesterday.*

Our home

WHEN THE estate agent first **showed** us **round** the flat, **my heart sank**. It looked fine from the outside, but inside it was in a pretty bad state. David, however, liked it, and as it was all we could afford, we eventually decided to buy it.

We **moved in** ▼ a couple of months later, and **set about doing** it **up**. We worked **flat out** to decorate the living room, kitchen and bedroom, and that **smartened** the place **up** quite a bit. We then had the old boiler **taken out** and **put in** a new one, which was both smaller and more efficient. My brother helped me to build a couple of cupboards to give us more storage space, and I **put up** some shelves for our books.

By this stage we had **settled in** and several neighbours had **invited** us **round**, so we soon **got to know** quite a few people in our building. The area also **turned out to be** a convenient place to live, as it has some decent shops and a good bus service. •

show sb round/around be a guide for sb when they visit a place for the first time.

my heart sank used to say that you suddenly felt very disappointed by sth.

set about (doing) sth start doing sth with energy and effort.

do sth up repair and decorate a home, etc.

flat out INF as quickly or with as much effort as possible. SYN like mad INF.

smarten sth/sb up make a place or person look neater or more attractive.

take sth out remove sth from a place where it is fixed or it belongs, e.g. a wallet from a pocket.

put sth in fix sth such as equipment in the place where it will be used.

put sth up build sth: *put up a building/shelves/a fence.*

settle in become familiar with a new home and start to feel comfortable there.

invite sb round/over ask sb to come to your home, usually for a drink or a meal.

get to know sb start to be familiar with sb and become friends.

turn out (to be sth) develop or end in a particular way, and often one that you did not expect.

WORD FOCUS

If you **move in,** or **move into sth**, you start to live in a new home. If you **move out,** or **move out of sth**, you leave your home forever. If you **move away**, you stop living in one place or area, and go to live in another.

Clothes shopping

The shop assistant brought me this pair of trousers to **try on**, but I couldn't **get into** them at all – I was really quite embarrassed. Then I realized she'd brought me the wrong size.

I saw a lovely top **the other day** that I thought would **go with** my red skirt. But when I tried it on, it just didn't look right.

Moira loves going to that little boutique in the High Street because they always **wrap** things **up** so beautifully.

When I **put on** the dress I bought last week, I realized it was actually too small. So, I **took** it **back** to exchange it for a bigger size, but they'd **sold out of** size 12.

If you**'re on the lookout for** a pair of sandals, it's worth **shopping around** at the moment, because there are a lot of bargains out there.

There's some nice stuff **on sale** in the market. I tried on a skirt, but it was a bit **on the tight side**: I couldn't **do** the zip **up.**

I tried on this lovely dress, but when I came out of the changing room, the shop assistant started laughing. I **had** it **on back to front**.

try sth on put on a piece of clothing, often in a shop, to see if it fits and how it looks.
get into sth put on a piece of clothing, especially with difficulty.
the other day recently.
go with sth look good in combination with sth.
wrap sth up cover sth, e.g. a present or parcel, completely in paper.
put sth on cover a part of your body with a piece of clothing or jewellery so that you are wearing it. OPP take sth off.
take sth back return to a shop with sth you have bought because it is broken or not suitable.
sell out (of sth) if a shop sells out of sth, it has no more of that particular thing left to sell.
be on the lookout for sth be trying to find or obtain sth.
shop around (for sth) go to several shops before you decide what particular thing to buy.
on sale if sth is on sale, it is available for people to buy.
on the big, small, tight, etc. side INF slightly too big, small, tight, etc.
do sth up fasten sth.
have sth on be wearing particular clothes, shoes, etc.
back to front (of clothing) with the back part at the front. (Also inside out = with the inside part facing out.)

Sleep

What kind of sleeper are you?

1 Do you usually **sleep like a log**?

2 Do you often have difficulty **dropping off to sleep**?

3 If you **wake up** during the night, do you often have difficulty **getting back to** sleep?

4 Do you often **toss and turn** during the night?

5 Do you usually use an alarm clock or your mobile phone to **wake** you **up**?

6 When your alarm **goes off** ▼, do you **get up** immediately?

7 Do you ever **sleep through** the alarm?

8 Do you ever **nod off** when you're watching TV?

9 Do you ever have **a lie-down** during the day?

10 Do you often have **a lie-in** at the weekend?

11 Do friends ever come and **sleep over** at your house?

12 Do you often **have a late night** at weekends?

sleep like a log sleep very well.
drop off (to sleep) INF start to sleep. SYN fall asleep.
wake up/wake sb up stop sleeping or stop sb else sleeping.
get back to sth return to a previous state or condition.
toss and turn be unable to sleep, or sleep badly, changing your position in bed all the time.
get up get out of bed after sleeping.
sleep through sth remain sleeping, even though sth around you is making a lot of noise.
nod off INF start to sleep, especially when sitting in a chair and when you do not intend to. SYN doze off.
a lie-down INF a short rest, especially on a bed: *have a lie-down.*
a lie-in INF a time when you stay in bed later than usual in the morning: *have a lie-in.* lie in V.
sleep over sleep at sb's house for one night (used especially about children staying with their friends). sleepover N.
have an early/a late night go to bed earlier/later than usual.

WORD FOCUS

If an alarm **goes off**, it rings (see text).
If somebody **goes off to sleep**, they start sleeping: *The baby's just gone off to sleep.*
If a light **goes off**, it stops working: *All the lights suddenly went off.*

Save or spend?

K9SIXTWO I'm interested to know if people still think it's worth trying to **save up for** the future. Or is it better just to spend what you've got?

SUGS As soon as I've **paid off** one or two debts, I want to save up for a deposit on a flat. I can't **go on living off** my parents, and I want to be able to **stand on my own feet**.

SMART With banks paying very little interest on savings, it makes more sense to **go out and** spend – at least **in the short term** ▼.

BABE I'm saving **like mad** at the moment, because I so need a holiday in the sun. **I've had enough of** the terrible summers in this country.

BJ I want to save enough to **pay my way** through university. I still need to **put aside** a few thousand, but it'll be worth it **in the long run** ▼.

SAL With inflation **going up** faster than salaries, what's the point of saving?

CAL I can only just about **live on** what I earn, so there's no point in me trying to save up for anything.

save up (for sth) keep money and not spend it, so that you can use it in the future.

pay sth off finish giving back to sb the money that you borrowed from them.

go on (doing sth) continue doing sth as before.

live off sb/sth depend on sb/sth for the money or food that you need.

stand on your own (two) feet behave in an independent way, especially by not asking for financial help from other people.

go out (and do sth) leave your home and go somewhere, especially to do sth enjoyable.

like mad INF very fast, hard, much, etc.

have had enough of sth INF used to say that you are tired or annoyed about a situation and want it to stop.

pay your way pay for everything yourself so that you do not depend on others.

put sth aside save or keep sth for future use. SYN put sth by.

go up increase; rise. OPP go down.

live on sth have enough money for the basic things you need to live.

WORD FOCUS

We use **in the short/long term** to refer to a time in the future, or the period of time leading to it, when we plan for or expect something to happen. (Also **in the short/long run**.)

How would you spend it?

If you **came into** some money, how would you spend it?

BEN: Well, it obviously **depends on** ▼ the amount you get. If it's a lot, the first thing I'd do is try to **keep quiet about** it. I wouldn't want everyone to know I was **rolling in money**.

To begin with, I'd want to **pay off** my debts, then I would think about **splashing out on** one or two things – maybe a better car and a bigger flat.

I would also want to **give** some of it **away**. I could **help out** my sister who is struggling financially with a small baby, and I'd look for a worthwhile charity that's **in need of** support. But as I said, I would try to do this **on the quiet**.

Finally, I would need to **put** money **by** for a later date. If I have any children, for example, I would want to be able to **invest in** their future – their education and so on. And **you never know** what money I might need for myself in the future.

come into sth receive money, land, etc. from someone who has died.
keep quiet about sth not tell anyone about sth.
rolling in money INF very rich.
to begin with used to introduce the first thing in a list of things that you are going to say. SYN for a start.
pay sth off finish giving back to sb the money that you borrowed from them.
splash out on sth INF buy sth expensive.
give sth away give sth to sb as a gift, or because you no longer want/need it.
help sb out help sb, especially by giving them money, or doing sth for them.
in need of sth needing sth.
on the quiet INF without telling anyone.
put sth by save or keep sth, especially money, for future use. SYN put sth aside.
invest in sth pay money into sth that you think will be useful in the future.
you never know used to say that sth may happen at some time in the future.

WORD FOCUS

Depend on sb/sth has different meanings:
1 be affected or decided by something (see text).
2 rely on somebody and be able to trust them: *I can depend on my family for help.*
3 need money, help, etc. from somebody: *She still depends on her parents for money.*

A waste of money

I told my brother that he'd **be better off** buying a flat. If he **carries on** renting, it's just money **down the drain**.

I **picked up** a couple of chairs in the antiques market for £150, but when I had them valued, I was told they were only worth £25 each. I **was** obviously **ripped off**.

I realized the meal would be expensive, but when I got the bill, it **came to** £250. I couldn't believe it.

I foolishly **put** £50 **on** a horse because a friend of mine told me it couldn't lose. Well, it did – in fact, it **came in** last.

The engineer said that if I **put in** underfloor heating, it would soon **pay for itself**. What a load of nonsense!

I knew that we were **paying over the odds** ▼ for that flat. The trouble is, when we sell it, we'll never **get** our money **back**.

be better off (doing sth) used to say that sb would be happier or more satisfied if they were in a particular position or did a particular thing. OPP be worse off (doing sth).

carry on (doing sth) continue doing sth.

down the drain INF if time, money or effort goes down the drain, it is wasted or lost.

pick sth up INF buy sth, especially cheaply or by chance.

rip sb off INF, OFTEN PASSIVE cheat sb, by making them pay too much for sth. rip-off N.

come to sth add up to sth.

put sth on sth gamble money on sth (gamble = risk money on a game, horse race, etc.).

come in finish a race in a particular position: *come in first/second/last*, etc.

put sth in fix equipment somewhere and connect it so that it can be used.

pay for itself if sth pays for itself, it saves you more money than it originally cost.

get sth back receive sth or have sth returned to you.

WORD FOCUS

If you **pay over the odds** for something, you pay more than usual or more than expected for it. If you **charge over the odds**, you make somebody pay more than usual or more than expected.

Living in poverty

How do people **on the breadline** manage during an economic recession?

MARY (pensioner)

I can just about **scrape by on** my pension, but I've had to **cut back on** ▼ gas and electricity, which have **gone through the roof** recently. But I won't be able to **make ends meet** if prices continue to **go up**.

DUNCAN (farm worker and father of four)

We were hoping to buy a car, but we've **used up** all that money on essentials – food and clothing for the kids. We used to **go away** most years too, but that**'s out of the question** now.

SCOTT (student)

I've had to **eat into** my savings just to have enough money to **live on**. My parents **help out** a bit, but if things get much worse, I'll have no option but to **run up** more debts – you've got to eat, haven't you?

on the breadline having very little money.

scrape by (on sth) manage to live on the money you have, but with difficulty.

go through the roof INF (of prices, etc.) increase quickly to a very high level.

make ends meet have just enough money to buy the things you need.

go up increase. OPP go down.

use sth up use all of sth so that there is none left.

go away leave your home for a period of time, especially for a holiday.

be out of the question used to say that sth is definitely not possible.

eat into sth gradually use money or a supply of sth that you were planning to save for another time or purpose.

live on sth have enough money for the basic things you need to live.

help (sb) out help sb, especially by giving them money or doing sth for them.

run sth up allow a bill, debt, etc. to reach a large total.

WORD FOCUS

If you **cut back on sth**, you reduce the amount of something that you use or the money that you spend. **cutback** N. If you **cut down on sth**, you reduce the amount of something that you eat, use or do: *I want her to cut down on her smoking.*

My best ever buy

My best ever buy has to be a set of Art Deco cups and saucers. I'd **been after** some for ages, then **one day**, I **came across** a whole set in absolutely fantastic condition. The owner even **knocked** 10% **off** because they'd been in her shop for ages and she couldn't **get rid of** them.

I'd been **shopping around** for some furniture for my study, when I heard that a factory nearby was **closing down** and **selling off** loads of stuff. I managed to **get hold of** an oak desk, an office chair and some bookshelves. I was **over the moon**.

A friend told me about a shop that was having a sale of leather goods, so we **went along**. But when we got there, they'd **sold out of** leather coats, which is what I really wanted. Anyway, I bought some leather boots instead, and they've been brilliant.

When I was a teenager, my older sisters and I **clubbed together** and bought a pony. They **don't come cheap**, but we'd always wanted one, and we all got Saturday jobs to help with the cost of **looking after** it.

be after sth be wanting or looking for sth.

one day on a particular day in the past. (It can also mean at some point in the future.)

come across sth find sth by chance, without planning it.

knock sth off INF reduce a price or a total by a particular amount.

get rid of sth sell, give away, or throw away sth that you no longer want or need.

shop around go to different shops before deciding what particular thing to buy.

close down if a company, shop, etc. closes down, it stops operating as a business.

sell sth off sell quantities of sth cheaply because you want to reduce the amount you have.

get hold of sth get sth that you need or want.

over the moon INF extremely happy.

go along go to attend an event.

sell out of sth if a shop sells out of sth, it has no more of that particular thing left to sell.

club together if people club together, each person gives some money so that the total amount can be used to buy sth.

sth does not come cheap sth is always expensive.

look after sth/sb care for sth/sb.

Getting around

Look out for a taxi with a light on – that means it's free.

I think the underground is probably the easiest way to **get around** the city.

We should **get in** soon. Let's **make our way** to the front of the train.

Excuse me. What time does the train **get into** Cambridge?

Could you **drop** me **off** just before the traffic lights, please?

Are we supposed **to hand in** our tickets when we leave the station?

Excuse me. Do we have to buy a ticket before we **get on** ▼ the bus?

The train leaves in half an hour, but we should **make it** if we **get a move on**.

We'll have to **look up** the times of the trains when we get to the station.

The train **was held up**, and I only just got to the airport **in the nick of time**.

look out for sth/sb try to find sth/sb. lookout N: *I've been on the lookout for a second-hand car.*

get around (sth) go or travel to different places within a city, country, etc.

get in (when travelling on a train or coach) arrive. If you get into sth, you arrive at a place.

make your way start moving towards a place.

drop sb (off) stop driving so that a passenger can get out of your car.

be supposed to do/be sth be expected or required to do/be sth because of a rule, custom or arrangement.

hand sth in give sth to a person in authority.

make it succeed in reaching a place, especially when it is difficult.

get a move on INF you tell sb to get a move on when you want them to hurry. SYN hurry up.

look sth up find information in a dictionary, timetable or reference book.

hold sth/sb up OFTEN PASSIVE cause a delay, or make sth/sb late. hold-up N.

in the nick of time INF at the very last moment.

WORD FOCUS

You usually **get on** a train, bus, plane, bike or motorbike. OPP **get off**. You **get in/into** a car or taxi. OPP **get out of sth**.

Road rage

I was **on my way** to work **the other day** when some idiot **cut** me **up** on the main road. It made me really angry, so I sounded the horn, and drove up right behind him. He just **drove on** ▼. Then he turned right, and I turned right; he turned left, and I turned left. I wasn't actually following him – I was just driving to work. At one point he **speeded up**, then immediately **slowed down** again, forcing me to **put on the brakes** really hard. This guy was **getting on my nerves**.

Of course, if I'd been **thinking straight**, I would've just told myself to **pull over** and **calm down**. But by this stage I'd **got myself** thoroughly **worked up** and pride was **kicking in**. I wasn't going to **give in** first. So, I stayed close behind. Then, he **took** me completely **by surprise**. When I reached my workplace, he **pulled in to** the car park in front of me and **got out of** the car. And for the first time I saw who it was: my boss! He'd been driving his wife's car because his was being serviced.

I'm now a lot calmer if someone **cuts in on** me when I'm driving. •

on my/the way going to or from a place.
the other day/week recently.
cut sb up suddenly drive in front of another vehicle in a dangerous way. SYN cut in (on sb).
speed up go faster. OPP slow down.
put sth on make a machine or piece of equipment start working; put on the brakes = make the car go more slowly.
get on sb's nerves do sth that annoys or irritates sb.
think straight think clearly and logically.
pull over (of a vehicle or its driver) move to the side of the road in order to stop or let sb pass.
calm down become more relaxed and less angry or anxious.
work yourself up OFTEN PASSIVE become very excited, upset or angry.
kick in INF begin to have an effect.
give in (to sb/sth) accept that you have been defeated by sb/sth.
take sb by surprise do sth that sb is not expecting.
pull in (to sth) (of a vehicle or its driver) move to the side of the road or the place mentioned and stop. OPP pull out (of sth).
get out (of sth) leave or climb out of a vehicle.

WORD FOCUS

If you **drive on**, you continue driving (see text). If you **drive off/away**, you drive the vehicle away and leave.

A long car journey

We **set off** just before 7.30, but the morning rush hour was already **building up**, so progress out of Bristol was quite slow. Eventually we got on the motorway heading south, but just after Junction 21, we **were held up** ▼ because of an accident, and traffic was **tailing back** ▼ for a couple of miles. We were stuck there for half an hour **or so**. By the time we **stopped off** for something to eat just after Exeter, we were way behind schedule, so we decided just to buy sandwiches and eat them while we **were on the move** – that way we **made up** a bit of **time**.

The next part of the journey was slightly better, though traffic **ground to a halt** when we got to Bodmin, as it often does. Anyway, we stopped there and **looked around** the town for a while, before **carrying on** to Zennor, our final destination. We'd rented a cottage outside the village. It was a bit **off the beaten track**, and the directions we were given took us down a couple of very narrow and windy lanes, but eventually we found it.

set off start a journey. SYN set out.
build up increase or make sth increase.
build-up N.
hold sb up OFTEN PASSIVE cause a delay or make sb late. hold-up N.
tail back (of traffic) form a long line that is not moving. tailback N.
or so used after a number, an amount, etc. to show that it is not exact.
stop off make a short visit somewhere during a longer trip in order to do sth.
be on the move be moving; be going somewhere.
make up (time) reduce time that has been lost.
grind to a halt slowly stop completely. SYN come/grind to a standstill.
look around/round (sth) walk round a place or building to see what is there.
carry on continue travelling or doing sth.
off the beaten track far away from other people, houses, etc.

WORD FOCUS

A number of phrasal verbs have related nouns. Some are written with a hyphen, e.g. **hold-up**; some are written without a hyphen, e.g. **tailback**. Another example related to transport and travel is **breakdown** (= a situation in which a vehicle or machine stops working). **break down** V: *We broke down on the motorway.* (See also 2.5.)

Airports

Departures

Arrivals →

↑ Check-in

My flight was at 8.30, so I had to get up **at the crack of dawn** in order to **check in**▼ by 7 o'clock.

It's lucky I checked in hours before **take-off,** because it took ages to **get through** all the security checks.

John and Julie's flight **takes off** at three, so if I leave work at lunchtime, I'll be able to get to the airport to **see** them **off**.

My parents **stopped over** in Singapore for a couple of nights, but they're **getting back** later today. I'm going to the airport to **pick** them **up**.

Airports **are murder** in July and August – it's almost inevitable you'll get delays **of one sort or another**.

I'd like to **take time off** at Easter, so I can **get away** for a few days. **As usual** though, I've left everything till **the last minute** – I hope the flights **aren't all booked up**.

at the crack of dawn very early in the morning.

take-off the moment when a plane leaves the ground. take off v.

get through sth proceed through sth or complete sth.

see sb off go to an airport or station with sb, in order to say goodbye to them.

stop over stay somewhere for a short time, e.g. one night, during a longer journey.

get back return, especially to your home.

pick sb/sth up go to a place and collect sb/sth, usually in a car.

be murder INF be difficult and unpleasant.

of one sort or another used to refer to different types of things, without saying exactly what you mean.

take (time, a week, etc.) off have a period of time away from work.

get away go somewhere in order to have a rest or a holiday.

as usual as happens most of the time.

the last minute the latest possible time for doing sth.

be booked up if a flight, hotel, etc. is booked up, there are no more seats, rooms, etc. available.

WORD FOCUS

If you **check in**, you go to a desk at an airport, hotel, etc., and tell sb officially you have arrived. **check-in** N. If you **check sth in**, you leave luggage with an official to be put on a plane or train.

A holiday break

AFTER A YEAR in which I'd been **rushed off my feet** at work, I decided I needed a complete break. I wanted a place where I could **get away from it all** – somewhere a bit **off the beaten track**.

I **ended up** in the Shetland Isles, which are 170 km north of mainland Scotland and probably the most remote place in the British Isles.

The climate isn't very hospitable, but it's a fascinating place, with archaeological sites **dating back** thousands of years, spectacular scenery, and enormous colonies of seabirds. To **get the most out of** it you really need to hire a car (the roads are quite good), and you can **get around** ▼ the different islands using the small car ferries.

I went to relax and **wind down**, but there was a surprising amount **going on**, and the people were very welcoming. It **made a** nice **change**, and I'm sure I'll **go back** again.

rushed off your feet extremely busy.
get away from it all INF go to a place where you are free from your usual work or responsibilities.
off the beaten track far away from other people, houses, etc.
end up find yourself in a place or situation that you did not plan to be in.
date back (to ...) have existed since a particular time in the past or for the period of time mentioned.
get sth out of sth enjoy sth, or learn or benefit from it.
wind down rest or relax after a period of activity.
go on USUALLY CONTINUOUS happen.
make a change used to say that an activity is enjoyable because it is different from what you usually do.
go back return.

WORD FOCUS

The phrasal verb **get around (sth)** has different meanings:
1 go to different places within an area (see text).
2 if **news gets around/round**, a lot of people hear about it: *News of the strike soon got around.*
3 if **you get around/round sth**, you find a way of either dealing with a problem or avoiding it: *People find ways of getting around the rules.*

A police investigation

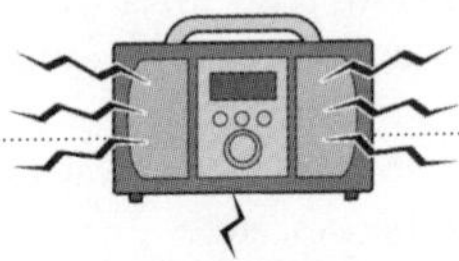

TWO MEN pretending to be gas engineers have **carried out** a series of robberies in the Branfield Park district of Bristol. The men knock on people's doors warning them of a gas leak, and ask if they can **check out** their gas appliances. Once the owner has **let** them **in**, one man distracts their attention by talking to them, while the other **goes through** drawers and cupboards **in search of** valuables. One resident told us that she **was** so completely **taken in** by the men that she even offered them money when they left – and that was after they had **walked off with** all her jewellery and nearly £500 in cash.

Police have now **put out** a warning in the area, telling people to **be on their guard**, and to **ask for** ▼ identification **at all times** if any stranger wants to enter their home for any reason. And they have tried to **impress upon** people that, **if in doubt**, they should simply explain that they are going to close the door while they **ring up** the company to check their identities. **Better to be safe than sorry.**

carry sth out do a planned activity or piece of work.
check sth out examine sth to be certain that it is correct, true or satisfactory.
let sb in allow sb to enter a house, room, etc.
go through sth search sth carefully.
in search of sth looking for sth.
take sb in OFTEN PASSIVE trick sb and make them believe sth that is not true.
walk off with sth INF steal sth.
put sth out publish or broadcast sth.
be on your guard be very careful and prepared for sth difficult or dangerous.
at all times always.
impress upon/on sb FML try to make sb understand how important sth is.
if in doubt = if you are not certain (used when giving advice to sb).
ring sb (up) telephone sb.
better (to be) safe than sorry used to say that you should behave carefully, even if this seems difficult or unnecessary, so that you will not have problems later.

WORD FOCUS

If you **ask for sth**, you speak or write to somebody because you want them to do something (see text).
If you **ask after sb**, you want news about them: *Michael was asking after you.*
If you **ask around**, you ask different people for information: *I don't know who can do the job, but I'll ask around.*

Crime headlines

POLICE **TIP-OFF** **LEADS TO** ARREST

Government to **tighten up** laws on gun control

Thieves **make off with** replica of giant panda

GOVERNMENT WILL **PUT A STOP TO** TAX FRAUD, SAYS PM

Footballer **let off** with a warning

Police issue new **crackdown** on knives

Teenagers **being led on** by gangs, says report

GOLF CLUB SAY THEY WILL **PRESS CHARGES**

Minister **in the clear** after enquiry

YOUNGSTERS **MIXED UP IN** VIOLENCE

Cyber crime **on the up**

Police to **phase out** tasers

FOOTBALL HELPS BOYS **STAY AWAY FROM** A LIFE OF CRIME

tip-off a piece of secret information that sb gives to sb, especially the police, to warn them about an illegal activity that is going to happen. tip sb off v.

lead to sth begin a process that causes sth to happen.

tighten sth up make a law, rule or system more strict.

make off with sth escape with sth, especially sth stolen.

put a stop to sth make sth stop happening, especially sth bad or unpleasant.

let sb off give sb little or no punishment for sth they did wrong.

crackdown (on sb/sth) a series of strong actions by the police or people in authority to stop or restrict an illegal activity. crack down on sb/sth v.

lead sb on INF encourage sb to do sth, especially by lying to them or promising them sth they cannot have.

press charges (against sb) officially accuse sb of committing a crime.

in the clear no longer believed to be guilty of sth illegal.

be/get mixed up in sth INF be or become involved in sth illegal or dishonest.

on the up increasing (see text) or improving.

phase sth out gradually stop using sth over a period of time. OPP phase sth in.

stay away from sth avoid becoming involved in sth.

A robbery

HIGH STREET ROBBERY

Passers-by in Broughton High Street were left shocked yesterday when two masked men **broke into** Hands the jeweller's, and **got away with** ▼ gems worth thousands of pounds.

The **break-in** took place early yesterday morning, shortly before the shop opened. Rob Chapman **takes up** the story: "I work in the newsagent's opposite the jeweller's, and I happened to notice two men **hanging around** the corner of Maple Street. I didn't think much of it until I heard the sound of glass smashing. **The next thing I knew**, the two men were taking jewellery out of the shop window and **running off with** it down one of the little alleys near the cinema. Someone from the shop **ran after** the robbers, but they managed to **get away** ▼."

People in the street said they were shocked that such a thing could happen **in broad daylight**, and one elderly man said he hoped the authorities would be **cracking down** much harder **on** crime in the area. The police say they **are** now **on the lookout for** two white men in their early to mid-twenties. ■

passer-by a person who is going past sth/sb by chance, especially when sth unexpected happens. pass by sb/sth V.

break into sth enter a building by force. break-in N.

take up sth continue a story or activity that you or sb else had begun.

hang around/about INF wait or stay near a place, not doing very much.

the next thing I knew used to say that a situation happened very quickly when you did not expect it.

run off with sth steal sth and quickly take it away.

run after sb run to try to catch sb.

in broad daylight used to say that a criminal or shocking event happens during the day when it can easily be seen.

crack down on sb/sth try harder to stop an illegal activity, and deal more strictly with the people responsible.

be on the lookout for sb be watching very carefully in order to find sb.

WORD FOCUS

Get away with sth has two meanings.
1 steal something and escape with it (see text).
2 do something wrong without being punished for it: *He's broken the law often, but he always gets away with it.*
If you **get away (from sb)**, you escape from a person (see text).

Incompetent criminals

A burglar was caught after he fell down a chimney while trying to **get away from** a house he had just **broken into**. Police arrested the 33-year-old after they **were called out** by the owners, who heard the burglar's cries for help.

A THIEF was arrested after he **left** his mobile phone **behind** at the scene of the crime. Rather stupidly, the burglar was **charging up** his phone in the victim's home when he was disturbed **rifling through** one of the rooms. Instinctively, he jumped out of a window to escape.

When police searched the victim's house, they found a mobile phone that didn't **belong to** anyone, so they rang one of the contact numbers and managed to **get hold of** the owner's name. That **resulted in** the man being arrested the next day.

TWO ARMED ROBBERS **held up** a security firm. They waited for the security van to pass them, then **went after** it and forced the driver to **pull over** ▼. They **made off with** the cash box, only to discover later that they had stolen the first aid kit!

get away from sth/sb escape from sth/sb.

break into sth enter a building by force, especially in order to steal things. (Also break in.) break-in N.

call sb out ask a person or an organization that provides a service to come and help you and deal with a problem.

leave sth behind not take sth with you when you go somewhere.

charge sth up pass electricity into the battery of a piece of electrical equipment so that it is stored there.

rifle through sth search sth quickly in order to find or steal sth.

belong to sb if sth belongs to you, you own it; it is yours.

get hold of sth obtain sth that you need or want.

result in sth cause sth or produce sth. SYN lead to sth.

hold sb/sth up steal from a person, business or vehicle by threatening them with a gun or other weapon. hold-up N.

go after sb/sth chase or follow sb/sth in order to catch or stop them.

make off with sth escape with sth, especially sth stolen.

WORD FOCUS

If a driver or vehicle **pulls over**, they slow down and then stop by the side of the road. If the police **pull sb over**, they ask the driver of a vehicle to slow down and stop by the side of the road.

Gang culture

GANG CULTURE claims the lives of many young men, so why do they **get caught up in** this violence? For some teenage boys, especially those who **do badly** in education, gangs offer money, excitement, girls and status. Some **turn to** gangs to **fill a gap** left by poor relationships with their own family, or even to **act out** the violence and abuse they may have suffered at home or elsewhere. The gang gives these boys their sense of identity.

For others, **belonging to** a gang simply offers protection. 'If you're **getting beaten up** and you're not part of them, you won't get help,' said one gang member.

Peer pressure can also play a part, with younger boys easily **led astray** when they **hang around with** older gang members. 'I **worked my way up**,' says one boy. 'The more stuff you do, the more ratings you get.' The 'stuff' includes stabbings, and often it is about revenge. 'When someone does something to you, you just want to **get** them **back**.'

The names of murdered teenagers **come up ▼ again and again**, as do the threats. And nobody should take them lightly. These guys **mean business**, and there seems no end in sight to the violence.

be/get caught up in sth be/become involved in sth unpleasant or undesirable.

do well/badly be successful/unsuccessful.

turn to sb/sth go to sb/sth for help, advice, support, etc.

fill a gap provide sth that is missing.

act sth out express your feelings about sth through your behaviour or actions.

belong to sth be a member of a club, an organization, etc.

beat sb up hit or kick sb hard, many times.

lead sb astray make sb behave badly.

hang around with sb INF spend a lot of time with sb.

work your way up move regularly to higher positions in an organization.

get sb back INF do sth to hurt or upset sb because they have done sth to hurt or upset you. (Also get back at sb.)

again and again used to say that sth happens many times.

mean business INF if sb means business, they seriously intend to do what they say they will do.

WORD FOCUS

Come up has many meanings.
1 be mentioned or discussed (see text).
2 If a problem **comes up**, it happens and needs to be dealt with: *I'm afraid I can't come tonight; something's come up.*
3 If something is **coming up** OFTEN CONTINUOUS, it is going to happen soon: *I've got an exam coming up next week.*

Using phones and mobiles

pick the phone **up** OPP **put** the phone **down** (also **hang up** = end the call)

switch the phone **on** SYN **turn** the phone **on** OPP **switch/turn** the phone **off**

plug the headset **in**

tap the number **in** / **punch** the number **in**

charge the phone **up**

scroll up OPP **scroll down**

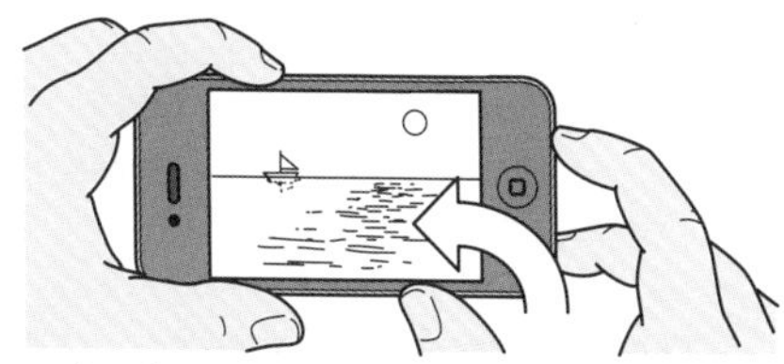

turn the phone **round/around**

a message **pops up** on the screen

Phone questionnaire

Tell us about your **phone experiences!**

- If you try to ring your bank, is it easy to **get through to** someone helpful?
- If you have a **pay-as-you-go** phone, do you ever forget to **top** it **up**?
- Does the battery ever **run out** while you're talking?
- Do you often **get cut off** when you're using a mobile?
- Do people often **ring** you **up out of the blue** to try and sell you something? If so, does it annoy you?
- When you ring up a big company, **are** you normally **put through to** the right person straightaway, or do they **put** you **on hold** for a long time?
- If someone leaves a voicemail asking you to **ring** them **back**, do you always do it?
- Do you have friends who **go on and on** and make it hard for you to **hang up**▼?
- Have you ever **hung up on** ▼ someone in the middle of a conversation?

get through to sb make contact with sb by phone.

pay-as-you-go a service for mobile phones where you pay for calls before you make them.

top sth up if you top up your mobile, you pay more money so that you can make more calls.

run out if the battery runs out, there is no electricity remaining in it.

cut sb off OFTEN PASSIVE if you get/are cut off, the phone call stops because the connection is broken.

ring sb (up) phone sb. SYNS give sb a call/ring, give sb a bell INF.

out of the blue suddenly and unexpectedly.

put sb through to sb connect sb to the person they want to talk to on the phone.

put sb on hold make a caller wait until the person they want to speak to is free.

ring sb back 1 phone sb who called you earlier (see text). 2 phone sb again. SYN call sb back.

go on (and on) (about sth/sb) talk about sth/sb for a long time, especially in a boring way.

WORD FOCUS

If you **hang up**, you end a phone call and put the phone down. SYN **ring off**. If you **hang up on sb** INF, you end a phone conversation suddenly without saying goodbye, perhaps because you are angry.

The downside of texting

In a recent survey **carried out** at two high schools in California, it was found that many teenagers were sending hundreds of texts a day **as a matter of course**. While this may be fun for teens interested in what is **going on** in their friends' lives, child care experts and parents are concerned that this type of activity may be **interfering with** children's sleep, **over and above** the usual sleep issues of this age group. What typically happens is that a question **pops into** their head just as they'**re about to** go to sleep, and they'**re on the phone** to a friend, who will then also be awake **until all hours** ▼.

Another issue is that adolescence is a time to begin to **break away from** your parents' influence as you **grow into** adulthood. However, mobile phones make it very easy to **stay in touch**, and many teenagers are texting their parents **all day long** ▼, to help them decide what to do in different situations, e.g. what shoes to buy, or how to do their homework. There **is** also **a question of** cost: some children can **run up** a huge bill for calls or texts, and will have to **pay** it **back** over time. Should parents be thinking of **cutting off** their children's phones?

carry sth out do a particular piece of work, research, etc.
as a matter of course/routine as a habit or as the usual way of doing things.
go on USUALLY CONTINUOUS happen.
interfere with sth stop sth from happening in the normal way.
over and above sth in addition to sth.
pop into sth if sth pops into your head/mind, you suddenly think of it.
be about to do sth be going to do sth very soon.
be on the phone be using the telephone.
break away (from sb) start to become more independent, especially from your parents.
grow into sth/sb develop into a particular type of person over a period of time.
stay/be/keep in touch be in contact with sb by often speaking or writing to them.
be a question of sth used to introduce an important issue in a situation.
run sth up if you run up a big bill, you owe a lot of money for sth.
pay sth back give sb the money you borrowed from them.
cut sth off stop the supply of sth.

WORD FOCUS

Until all hours means until very late at night.
All day/week/year long means for the whole day/week/year: *Yesterday it rained all day long.*

Domestic robots

We **are on the cusp** of a robot revolution – one which **has** a lot **in common with** the computer revolution of the 80s and 90s. Could robots **make a difference** to our lives? You only have to think about the rapidly ageing population and how we will **care for** them in the future. Could robots **make up for** the shortages in the number of carers we will need in years **to come**? So far, robots have **turned out to be** too expensive to own, but they could **be hired out** and still be cheaper than humans.

But what could they do? **First and foremost**, they could **carry out** many tasks that we **take for granted**, but which the elderly find increasingly hard – such as cleaning or fetching things. They could also **play a role in** the health of the elderly by **keeping track of** their medicines, or by helping an elderly person to **call in** a doctor or human carer in an emergency. But the real problem is whether we will be prepared to **hand over** our lives to a robot.

be on the cusp of sth be at a time when a situation or state is going to change.

have sth in common with sth (of things, places, etc.) have the same features as sth else.

make a difference have an important effect on sb/sth, especially a good effect.

care for sb look after sb who is sick, very old, very young, etc. SYN take care of sb.

make up for sth do sth that corrects a bad situation; compensate for sth.

to come USED AFTER A NOUN in the future: *in days/weeks/years to come.*

turn out (to be sth) be shown or be found to be sth, especially after a period of time.

hire sth out let sb use sth, e.g. a car or machine, temporarily in return for money.

first and foremost used to emphasize the most important point, reason, etc. for sth.

carry sth out do and complete a task.

take sth for granted expect that sth will always happen in a particular way, and not think about how important or useful it is.

play a role/part in sth be involved in sth, especially in a way that is important.

keep track of sth pay attention to sb/sth, so that you know what is happening to them.

call sb in ask for the help or services of sb, e.g. a doctor, the police.

hand sth over give power or control over sth to another person.

Computers

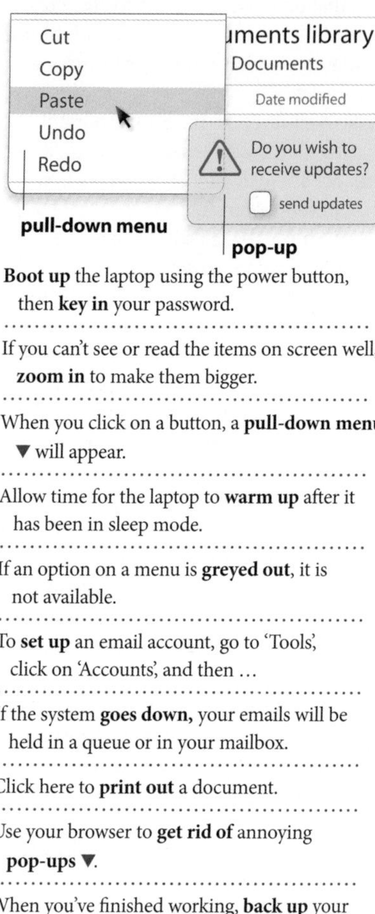

Boot up the laptop using the power button, then **key in** your password.

If you can't see or read the items on screen well, **zoom in** to make them bigger.

When you click on a button, a **pull-down menu** ▼ will appear.

Allow time for the laptop to **warm up** after it has been in sleep mode.

If an option on a menu is **greyed out**, it is not available.

To **set up** an email account, go to 'Tools', click on 'Accounts', and then …

If the system **goes down,** your emails will be held in a queue or in your mailbox.

Click here to **print out** a document.

Use your browser to **get rid of** annoying **pop-ups** ▼.

When you've finished working, **back up** your files, **log off** and then **shut down** your PC.

boot (sth) up COMPUTING start a program that makes a computer ready to use. SYN start (sth) up.

key sth in put information into a computer using a keyboard.

zoom in make the area of a text or a picture on a screen larger. OPP zoom out.

warm up (of a machine) become ready to use after you switch it on.

greyed out if part of a computer screen is greyed out, the writing appears in a dull colour to show that you cannot use it.

set sth up arrange for sth to happen.

go down stop working for a period of time.

print sth out/off produce a copy on paper of a document on a computer. printout N.

get rid of sth take action to stop sth that is annoying you or causing problems.

back sth up make a copy of the files that you have created on your computer. backup N.

log off/out stop using a computer system by giving it particular instructions. OPP log on/in.

shut (sth) down if you shut down a computer, or it shuts down, it stops operating.

WORD FOCUS

Some phrasal verbs have associated phrasal nouns or adjectives: **pull down a menu**, a **pull-down menu** (see picture); **pop up**, a **pop-up** / a **pop-up window** (see picture); **print sth out**, a **printout**, etc.

Talking about the news

*The story **leaked out** via Twitter.*	leak out (of secret information) become known to the public. SYN get out.
*Our reporter is **following up** a lead on the missing child case.*	follow sth up find out more about sth that sb has told you. (lead = some information that may help to solve a crime.)
*The journalist believed there was a deliberate **cover-up**.*	cover-up an attempt to stop people from discovering the truth, especially about a crime or serious error. cover sth up V.
*The reporter **was tipped off** about the government's secret tax plans.*	tip sb off give sb, e.g. the press or the police, a secret warning or piece of information. tip-off N.
*The press are **digging around** for information about the family.*	dig around try hard to find out secret or private information about sb.

*The story has **been blown up out of all proportion** by the media.*	blow sth up out of (all) proportion make a situation seem much worse than it really is.
*The victim **opened up to** the journalist.*	open up to sb begin to talk more about what you feel and think.
*The latest news has **cast doubt on** the footballer's allegations.*	cast doubt on sth make sth seem less certain or true.
*I spoke to the editor **off the record**.*	off the record said to sb in private and not intended to be made public. OPP on the record.
*It says in the paper that negotiations are continuing **behind the scenes**.*	behind the scenes secretly rather than in public.
*The paper didn't **check out** the facts.*	check sth out find out if sth is true or correct.
*Do they **put across** the views of the newspaper's owner?*	put sth across communicate an opinion or idea to other people.

Newspaper headlines

TRIBUTES PAID TO MOTORWAY CRASH VICTIMS

Beyoncé **gives birth to** baby girl

Council to **stamp out** illegal DVD sales

SHELL **GETS THE GO-AHEAD** FOR MASSIVE NORTH SEA PROJECT

PRESIDENT **RULES OUT** EARLY PARLIAMENTARY ELECTIONS

Prime Minister **speaks out in favour of** mixed marriage

Trouble **flares up** ▼ at London anti-cuts demonstration

RECOVERY IN HOUSE PRICES **WIPED OUT** BY NEW ECONOMIC RECESSION

PRICE OF GOLD **LEVELS OFF** AFTER WEEK-LONG RALLY

Arsenal owner promises to **stick by** manager

TWO STATE OFFICIALS **STEP DOWN** AMID SCANDAL

Post Office **brings out** new stamps to honour local heroes

Police **looking into** daytime burglaries

pay tribute to sb say or do sth to show your respect or admiration for sb.
give birth to sb/sth produce a baby or young animal.
stamp sth out use force or strong action to stop or prevent sth that is bad, dangerous or unpleasant. SYN put a stop to sth.
get the go-ahead get permission to do sth. (Also give sb the go-ahead.)
rule sth out decide that sth is not possible.
speak out (about/against sth) give your opinion strongly and in public about sth, especially to protest against or defend sth.
in favour of sth showing you support sth or agree with it.
wipe sth out remove or destroy sth completely.
level off/out stay at a steady level of development after big rises or falls.
stick by sb continue to support sb who is in a difficult situation.
step down/aside leave an important job and let sb else take your place.
bring sth out produce or publish sth.
look into sth investigate or examine sth.

WORD FOCUS

Flare up has several meanings.
1 If trouble **flares up**, people suddenly become angry, violent, etc. (see text).
2 If an illness **flares up**, it starts again.
3 If a fire **flares up**, it suddenly starts burning more brightly.

Press behaviour

The phone hacking scandal

IN 2007, two British journalists were jailed for **hacking into** the phones of celebrities, **listening in on** their messages and publishing stories based on the information they had gathered. However, this was **by no means** the end of the story. In 2011, a crisis **blew up** at the *News of the World* newspaper, with further revelations of phone hacking **relating to** people **in the public eye** ▼, and to those who had been victims of crime, including two shocking and famous cases of couples whose children had been murdered. This caused widespread revulsion among the public, not just because hacking is **against the law**, but also because of the poor ethical standards of the press. The newspaper **was closed down** immediately, and the government announced a public enquiry.

The scandal has shown the media **in a bad light**, and there have been calls for press regulations to **be tightened up**. However, politicians and the police **are** also **in the firing line** for **dragging their heels** over the affair, and being too close to the media in order to get good publicity. All three institutions need to **redeem themselves in the eyes of** ▼ the public.

hack (into) sth secretly connect to sb's mobile phone or computer to find or change information on it.
listen in on sth/sb listen to sb else's private conversation.
by no means (used for emphasis) not at all; certainly not.
blow up (of a problem, crisis, etc.) start suddenly.
relate to sth be connected with sth.
against the law not permitted by law.
close sth down stop a business operating.
in a good/bad light if you see or show sth in a good, bad, etc. light, it seems good, bad, etc.
tighten sth up make a rule or law more strict.
be in the firing line be in a position where people can criticize you or blame you.
drag your heels/feet be deliberately slow in doing sth or making a decision.
redeem yourself do sth good when you have behaved badly, so that people will think well of you again.

WORD FOCUS

Many idioms are based around eyes.
1 in the public eye = well known to many people through newspapers and TV (see text).
2 in sb's eyes/in the eyes of sb = according to what somebody thinks or feels (see text).
3 keep your eyes open (for sth) = watch carefully in case something happens.

Film reviews

'It's hard to know what to **make of** Joe Rowson's latest film, but **in brief**, it fails to **come up to** his usual high standards …

The book was brilliant, but the film doesn't really **live up to** expectations, and casting a footballer as the leading actor **was asking for trouble** …

A film that **caters for** the whole family, and **judging by** the audience's reaction it will do well at the box office …

The opening sequence was quite dull and **reminded** me **of** so many other films. It really only **comes alive** when Cruise meets his co-star …

The film **is** badly **let down** by the poor acting, and casting Ana Heaven as a working-class mother is **hard to swallow** …

The success of this film **hinges on** the quality of the acting, which is superb …

Remakes of much-loved movies are a challenge, and sadly, this is **nothing like as** good **as** the previous version. The film seems to **peter out** at the end as if the director had **run out of steam**.'

make sth of sth/sb if sb asks you what you make of sth/sb, they are asking for your impression or opinion of sth/sb.
in brief in a few words, without details.
come up to sth reach an acceptable level or standard.
live up to sth be as good as what was expected or promised. (In this case, people expected to like the film because the book was good, but they didn't.)
be asking for trouble INF if you are asking for trouble, you are doing sth silly or dangerous.
cater for sb/sth provide what is needed for a particular group of people.
judging by sth used to say that you think sth is true based on what you have seen, heard or learnt. SYN going by sth.
remind sb of sth make sb remember sth that they have seen, read or experienced.
come alive become interesting and exciting. SYN come to life.
let sth down make sth less successful than it should be.
hard to swallow difficult to accept or believe.
hinge on sth depend on sth completely.
nothing like as … as INF not at all as … as, not nearly as … as.
peter out gradually become smaller or weaker and then come to an end.
run out of steam INF lose energy and enthusiasm.

The pros and cons of TV

DISCUSSION:
What's good and bad about TV?

JOANNA Watching TV **eats into** your day. People should **take the plunge**, **switch** it **off** and **get on with their lives**!

MARISOL My dad**'s glued to** the TV all day long. The trouble is, he's getting fat because he's just behaving like a **layabout**, watching TV and eating loads of crisps. Stop it!!!

RUPERT TV **draws** you **in** – it's addictive. You just **get used to** ▼ sitting there, **night after night**. Fortunately I've stopped now; it was starting to **get in the way of** my relationships with my family.

ASHOK **I've got nothing against** TV, but I think there are more worthwhile things people can be doing with their time.

RAMONA I love TV! I've acquired lots of new skills from programmes, I watch and learn from current affairs programmes, and I find it a great way to **wind down** after the working day.

JAMEELA I think TV can **broaden your horizons** – especially the documentaries and travel programmes. I really believe it has **opened up** the world for me.

eat into sth use up part of sth, especially sb's time or money.

take the plunge decide to do sth that is hard or important after thinking about it.

switch sth off make sth stop working.

get on with your life stop doing sth or worrying about sth and start living a normal life again.

be glued to sth INF be looking at sth and not paying attention to anything else.

layabout INF a lazy person who avoids work. lie about/around v.

draw sb in involve sb in a situation, often when they do not want to take part.

night after night every night for a long period of time.

get in the way of sth prevent sth from developing successfully.

have (got) nothing against sth/sb have no reason to dislike sth/sb.

wind down relax or rest after a period of activity.

broaden your horizons make you see a wide range of opportunities and choices.

open sth up create new possibilities or opportunities for sb.

WORD FOCUS

If you **get used to doing sth**, it becomes familiar because you have done it several times already. Do not confuse this with **used to do sth**. If you **used to** play football, for example, you played often in the past, but you no longer play.

TV crime series

Law & Order

WHEN DICK WOLF was first working on a new television crime series in 1988, he initially **toyed with** the idea of calling it *Night & Day*, but then **hit upon** the title *Law & Order*.

The show follows a two-part approach. The first half opens with a crime, and then a police investigation. Detectives **come up with** various theories about the crime, and **piece together** the evidence before they arrest and charge a suspect. They then **hand over** to the prosecutors, and the second half of the show **centres around** the trial of the defendant. It was also decided **early on** to **base** the show **on** real life cases which were **making the headlines**.

Wolf took the idea to one of the TV bosses, who **pointed out** that the series resembled an earlier 1960s TV show called *Arrest and Trial*. However, after a couple of false starts, the crime series finally **got off the ground** on September 13, 1990. It was a huge success and continued for 20 years before it finally **ran out of steam.** The last episode of the series **went out** on May 24, 2010.

toy with sth consider sth, but not seriously or in a definite way: *toy with the idea of doing sth.*

hit on/upon sth think of a good idea suddenly or by chance.

come up with sth find or produce an idea, an answer, etc.

piece sth together understand a situation, story, etc. by taking all the facts and details and putting them together.

hand (sth) over (to sb) give another person the responsibility for sth.

centre around/round sth/sb if sth centres around sb/sth, they are the main subject of attention or interest.

early on in the early part of a process or activity.

base sth on sth use an idea, a fact or a situation as the point from which sth can be developed.

make the headlines be an important item of news in newspapers, on the radio or on TV.

point sth out (to sb) mention sth in order to give sb information about it or make them notice it.

get (sth) off the ground start happening successfully (or make sth start happening successfully).

run out of steam INF lose energy and enthusiasm and stop doing sth, or do it less well.

go out when a radio or TV programme goes out, it is broadcast or shown.

Hobbies

How to choose a hobby

WHY? **For a start**, what do you want to **get out of** a hobby? Is it a new skill? A way to meet people? Or just something to **while away** the time?

WHAT? Do a bit of research on possible hobbies. **Keep an open mind** and don't **rule** things **out** without giving them some thought. You may be attracted to a hobby that **has something to do with** your existing skills, or **a change of direction**.

TIME? You will need to **take into account** the amount of time you can **devote to** a hobby. Are you generally very busy, or do you **have** a lot of **time on your hands**? Some hobbies are easy to **pick up where you left off**, even after a long break, whereas others may **take up** more of your time or require regular practice.

COST? Another factor is the amount of money you can spend. While some of the best things in life are often free, others come **at a price**. Be prepared to **do your homework** and find out how much you will be **letting yourself in for**, before you **commit yourself to** an expensive hobby such as learning to fly, owning a horse or sailing.

Whatever you choose, good luck!

for a start used to introduce the first point in a series.

get sth out of sth enjoy or benefit from sth.

while (time) away spend time in a pleasant, lazy way.

keep/have an open mind be willing to listen to or accept new ideas.

rule sth out decide that sth is not possible or suitable.

be/have something to do with sth be connected to sth.

a change of direction a situation in which sb starts doing sth completely new or different.

take sth into account consider certain facts or circumstances when making a decision.

devote sth/yourself to sth spend a lot of time or effort doing sth.

have time on your hands INF have little to do; not be busy.

pick sth up where you left off start sth again from the point where you stopped.

take up sth fill or use an amount of time or space.

at a price costing a lot of money.

do your homework prepare for sth by learning as much about it as you can.

let yourself in for sth INF put yourself in a difficult situation.

commit yourself to (doing) sth say that you will do or be involved in sth, so that it is then difficult not to do it.

My free time

CATHY: I **took up** marathon running five years ago. I'd just **got over** some health problems, and my doctor advised me to **start off** with some light running. Eventually I **went in for** a few races and, to my amazement, I **walked off with** ▼ two medals; that **spurred** me **on to** try the longer races. Marathons **take a lot out of** you, but I've never been happier.

SEAN: My hobby's a bit unusual: it's Latin American dancing. It was my girlfriend who **talked** me **into** it – she'**s mad keen on** dancing. We went to a free introductory class to **try** it **out** and loved it, so we **signed up for** the course. It's really hard **to start with**, but if you **stick at** it, you gradually **pick up** the steps, and once you've got them, the variations **come easily**. It's fun and it keeps you **in shape**.

take sth up start doing a hobby or following an interest regularly.
get over sth become well or happy again after an illness, shock, separation, etc.
start off begin by doing sth.
go in for sth enter a competition or race, or take an exam.
spur sb on (to do sth) encourage sb to do sth or try harder to achieve sth.
take a lot/it out of sb need a lot of effort and make sb feel very tired.
talk sb into (doing) sth persuade sb to do sth. OPP talk sb out of (doing) sth.
be mad keen on sth INF be extremely enthusiastic about sth.
try sth out do sth or experience sth in order to see if you like it.
sign up for sth agree to take part in a course of study or series of classes.
to start with at the beginning.
stick at sth continue to work in a serious or determined way to achieve sth.
pick sth up learn a skill, often by watching or listening to other people.
come easily if sth comes easy/easily, it is not difficult to learn or to do.
in shape in good physical condition. OPP out of shape.

WORD FOCUS

Walk off with sth INF has two meanings:
1 win something easily (see text).
2 steal something: *He walked off with my coat!*

Reading

As a child, I did really badly at school, but my love of reading **made up for** my lack of formal education. You'd often find me **curled up** on the sofa with a book in my hand. Dad was always **going on at** me for not helping Mum, but I was far happier **immersed in** a gripping story than tidying my bedroom.

I **feel sorry for** people who don't enjoy reading, because they are **missing out on** so much. A good story **captures your imagination**, and the pleasure that you **derive from** a great book stays with you forever.

I love thrillers – when a new book **comes out** by Henning Mankell or John Grisham, I have to **get hold of** ▼ it **right away**. I'm currently reading a brilliant book by John Le Carré – I just **can't put it down**.

Of course, some books are harder to **get into**, but I usually find that it's worth it, because in the end, it **pays off** – maybe because I **relate to** the characters, or I learn something, or things **turn out** in an unusual way. You can't beat a good book.

make up for sth make a bad situation better or compensate for sth that has been lost.
curl up lie or sit with your arms and legs bent close to your body.
go on at sb INF criticize sb regularly and for a long time.
immerse yourself/sb in sth become completely involved in sth.
feel sorry for sb feel sympathy for sb because they are in a bad situation.
miss out (on sth) lose an opportunity to do or have sth.
capture sb's imagination make sb interested in or excited about sth.
derive sth from sth FML get sth, such as a product or an advantage, from sth else.
come out (of a book, film, etc.) become available to buy or see.
right away immediately.
can't put sth down cannot stop reading sth because it is so good.
get into sth start enjoying sth or being interested in it.
pay off bring a good result.
relate to sb feel that you understand sb's situation and have sympathy with it.
turn out develop or end in a particular way.

WORD FOCUS

Get hold of sth means to get something that you need or want (see text). If you **get hold of sb**, you manage to talk to them on the phone or in person.

Art galleries with children

If you're planning to take young children to an art gallery, it's important to **plan ahead**.

Choose an exhibition that you think will **go down well with** them, but don't **shy away from** subjects just because you don't like them. It's a good idea to **read up about** the exhibition before you go, and to encourage the children to look at the gallery's website, but not so much that it **turns** them **off**. **Printing out** a few paintings for them to find in the gallery may help.

Try to avoid times when the gallery will be very busy. Once you are there, tell the children to **keep their voices down**, but talk to them quietly about the pictures **on display**. Encourage them to let their imaginations **run riot** ▼ by pretending that they are in the painting. Museums often **lay on** short tours for kids, and it's a good idea to join one. Most staff will be happy to **engage with** them and answer their questions.

In the gallery shop, let the children **pick out** postcards of pictures to **remind** them **of** their visit. Later at home, you can do **follow-up** activities with them, such as writing their thoughts on the back of the cards, or doing their own paintings.

plan ahead think about and plan for the future. (Also think/look ahead.)
go down well/badly (with sb) get a particularly good/bad reaction from sb.
shy away from sth avoid doing or getting involved with sth because you are not confident enough, or are worried about it.
read up about/on sth read about a subject in order to get information.
turn sb off (sth) make sb feel bored with or not interested in sth. turn-off N, INF.
print sth out/off produce a paper copy of a computer document.
keep your voice down speak quietly (often used as an instruction).
on display if sth is on display, it is put in a place where people can look at it.
lay sth on INF provide sth for sb, especially entertainment, service, food, etc.
engage with sb FML communicate with sb.
pick sth out choose one thing or person from a group.
remind sb of sth make sb remember sth that they have seen, read or experienced.
follow-up an action or activity that continues sth that has already started. follow sth up V.

WORD FOCUS

If your imagination **runs riot**, you let it develop in a lively way without trying to control it. However, if people, children, etc. **run riot**, they are noisy, out of control and possibly violent.

Board games

S₁ C₃ R₁ A₁ B₂ B₂ L₄ E₁

Have you ever **tried your hand at** Scrabble? It's a board game **based on** chance and strategy, and it also **calls for** a certain language ability. In recent times it has **been turned into** an online game and is played worldwide.

In the game, letter tiles **are jumbled up** in a bag, from which you take seven. You have to **make up** words of between two and seven letters, which you lay on the board to win points. You then **count up** your score for that word and the total **is noted down** on a sheet of paper. You replace the tiles that you have **put down** with the same number from the bag.

The next player has to add a word, but he or she must use one of the letters already on the board. Players **take turns to** ▼ add words; if they cannot make a word, they can **put** the letters **back** and take some new ones. The game ends when all the letters have **been used up**, and one player has **run out of** letters. The other players will have some letters remaining; the points for these **are added up** and **taken away from** their final score.

try your hand at sth do an activity for the first time to see if you like it or are good at it.
base sth on sth use an idea as the starting point from which sth can be developed.
call for sth need or require sth.
turn sth into sth make sth become sth different.
jumble sth up mix things together in an untidy way, without any order.
make sth up form sth from a number of parts.
count sth up calculate the total number of things or people in a group.
note sth down write sth down so that you will have a record of it.
put sth down place sth on a surface. (In this case, put letters on the board.)
put sth back put sth in the place where it was before it was moved.
use sth up use all of a supply of sth.
run out of sth if you run out of sth, you use all of it and have nothing left.
add sth up calculate the total of two or more numbers or amounts.
take sth away (from sth) subtract or remove a number from another number.

WORD FOCUS

If people **take turns to do sth**, or **take it in turns to do sth**, they do it one after the other so that everyone has the chance to do it. This often happens in games.

Phrases in team sports

The team should be ***at full strength*** *on Saturday.*

at full strength playing with all the best players in your team. OPP below strength.

Powell is only just back from injury, so he's ***on the bench****.*

on the bench a player who is on the bench for a match is a substitute (= a player who can replace another member of the team during the match).

The game ***kicks off*** *at 2.30.*

kick off (of a football or rugby match) start. kick-off N.

We ***lost the toss*** *and we're playing against the wind in the first half.*

lose the toss guess wrongly which side of a coin will face upwards when it lands on the ground. OPP win the toss.

The referee ***sent*** *the player* ***off*** *for a two-footed tackle.*

send sb off order a player who has broken a rule to leave the field of play and not return.

*We **got knocked out** in the semi-final of the Cup last year.*	knock sb out if you knock sb out of a competition, you defeat them and they no longer take part in it. (Also, a knockout competition.)
*We **came close to** scoring at the end.*	come close to doing sth almost do sth.
*They managed to score, but it was **against the run of play**.*	against the run of play if a team scores against the run of play, they score when the other team had a better chance of scoring.
*We **were on top** throughout the first half.*	be on top be in a leading position or in control of a match, competition, etc.
*In the end we **went down** 2-1 **to** the German team.*	go down (to sb) lose to sb in a competition, especially in sport.
*We're **playing at home** next week.*	play at home if a team plays at home, it plays in the town, city, etc. that it comes from. OPP play away.

Winter sports

Keep safe and have fun!

❄ **No matter what** sport you do, there are two golden rules in winter sports: use the right equipment, and **wrap up** warm.

❄ This may seem strange for a winter sport, but remember that sunlight is reflected off the bright snow back into your face, so **play it safe** and **cover up** with sunscreen.

❄ When you're sledding, be sure to **sit up** rather than **lie down**. Lying down increases the risk of injury. And if you're **trying out** a new hill, walk it first to check for obstacles.

❄ When you're skating, **stick to** approved ice. **Under no circumstances** ▼ should you try skating on ice that hasn't been approved, even for a second. And it **makes sense** to skate in the same direction as everyone else, otherwise you might **bump into** people.

❄ When you're skiing, **watch out for** others to avoid collisions.

no matter what/how/where, etc. used to say that sth is always true, whatever the situation, or that sb should certainly do sth.

wrap up wear enough clothes to keep you warm: *wrap up warm.*

play (it) safe be careful; avoid risks.

cover up put sth on all or part of your body to hide it, protect it, or keep it warm.

sit up get or be in a sitting position, not lying down or leaning back: *sit up straight.*

lie down be in a position in which your body is flat on a surface, e.g. on a bed.

try sth out test sth to see what it is like and whether it is suitable or effective.

stick to sth continue doing or using sth, and not change or stop it.

make sense be practical and sensible.

bump into sb/sth accidentally hit against sb/sth.

watch out (for sth) pay attention so that you see if anything bad or unusual happens.

WORD FOCUS

Under/in no circumstances is used to emphasize that something should never happen or be allowed.
In/under the circumstances is used to show that we have thought about the conditions that affect a situation: *Under the circumstances, I decided not to go to the wedding.*

The rise of a great tennis player

NOVAK DJOKOVIC had always been a fine player, but until 2010, was never **on a par with** Roger Federer or Rafael Nadal. Then he started to **build up** his strength and fitness, and somehow developed a new-found mental toughness. This was clearly **on display** in the semi-final of the US Open in 2011. Match point down in the fifth set, Djokovic **gambled on** a massive service return and it **came off** ▼. He won the point and **went on to** win the match.

Having lost five games **in a row** against Djokovic, Nadal was determined to win the final. But he **got off to a bad start**, losing the first two sets. He **came back** in the third, winning 7-6 on a tie-break, but the recovery was short-lived. Djokovic took control **from the outset of** the fourth set, and won the match quite comfortably.

The question remaining now is whether Djokovic can **keep up** this phenomenal run, or whether Nadal will **fight back** and regain the number one position.

on a par (with sb/sth) at about the same level or standard as sb/sth.

build sb/sth up make sb/sth bigger, stronger, fitter, etc.

on display if a skill, quality, etc. is on display, it is clear and easy to notice.

gamble on sth take a risk with sth, hoping it will bring you success.

go on to do sth do sth after completing sth else.

in a row one after another, without anything different happening in between.

get off to a good/slow/bad, etc. start start sth well/slowly/badly, etc.

come back become successful or effective after being in a bad situation, especially in a sports event. comeback N.

from/at the outset (of sth) from/at the beginning of sth.

keep sth up maintain sth at the same level or standard.

fight back work hard to achieve or oppose sth, especially in a situation where you are losing. fightback N.

WORD FOCUS

If something **comes off**, it is successful, often when it has been risky or difficult, or when it is surprising (see text). We also use **come off** when a player leaves a sports field and is replaced by another player: *Rooney came off after an hour, and was replaced by Hernandez.*

Sports injuries

Avoiding sports injuries

First and foremost ▼ don't start playing a sport if you are badly **out of shape**. You need to be in reasonably good condition before you even start a sport, otherwise you risk injury.

You also need to understand exactly what you'**re meant to do** in any given sport, and to **abide by** the rules, as they are there to ensure your safety **in the first place** ▼. And if a sport requires equipment **such as** helmets and gum shields, make sure you wear them. This is absolutely essential if you **take part in** any sport that involves a lot of physical contact; safety must **come first** ▼.

Some people like to train every day in the belief that it will make them better. In fact, this may increase the likelihood of injury. You should **build** regular rest periods **into** your training routine to **cut down** the risk of injury, and when you play, always **warm up** and **warm down**. Do some stretching exercises to **loosen up**, and then after a game to warm down.

Finally, don't play when you're injured, or **come back** too soon after an injury; you then **run a risk of** a more serious injury.

out of shape in bad physical condition. OPP in shape.

be meant to do sth if you are meant to do sth, you should do it because of a rule or an agreement.

abide by sth FML accept and act according to a law, an agreement, etc.

such as used to introduce more examples of the type of thing or person that you have just mentioned.

take part (in sth) be involved in an activity with other people.

build sth into sth make sth a permanent part of a system, plan, etc.

cut sth down reduce sth.

warm up prepare for a sport or activity by doing gentle exercises. warm-up N. SYN loosen up.

warm down do gentle exercises to relax your body after doing a particular sport or activity. warm-down N.

come back return to playing.

run a/the risk of sth/doing sth be or put yourself in a situation in which sth bad could happen to you.

WORD FOCUS

There are different idioms using 'first':
first and foremost most importantly; more than anything else.
in the first place used to state the most basic reason for sth.
come first be the most important person or thing.

The mind of a champion

Olympic, world and European champion track cyclist Victoria Pendleton is **a force to be reckoned with**. But she is also sensitive and surprisingly vulnerable for someone who has **devoted herself to** competing in such a tough sport. 'I hate the idea of **letting** people **down** – and when I do I feel such a failure,' she says.

In some respects, it is the fear of failure that motivates her and makes her **keep going** when many others would **give up**.

'Maybe guys have these insecurities, but they **keep it to themselves**. I can't do that.'

Pendleton is prepared to **open up** ▼ and let others see her vulnerability, and she tries to **switch off** between races by watching episodes of her favourite TV shows. But in the **build-up to** races, competitiveness and ambition **take over**. Of her 2008 Olympic final, she says: 'I was **drawing on** a lot of negative resentment, thinking, "**I'll show you**". That's how I felt on the inside. I think now: "Is that really me?"'

a force to be reckoned with a person whose ability or influence deserves to be respected.

devote yourself to sth spend a lot of time or effort doing sth.

let sb down make sb disappointed by not doing sth that they expected you to do.

keep going continue to do sth even though it is difficult.

give up stop doing sth that you have been trying to do because it is too difficult.

keep sth to yourself not tell other people about sth.

switch off INF stop thinking about sth or paying attention to sth, especially as a way of relaxing.

build-up (to sth) the time before an event when people are talking about it and preparing for it.

take over (from sth) become bigger or more important than sth else; replace sth.

draw on/upon sth use a supply of sth that is available to you.

I'll show you used to talk about what you intend to do as an angry reaction to what sb has said or done.

WORD FOCUS

If you **open up (to sb)**, you talk about your personal feelings and experiences. If you **bottle sth up**, you do not allow other people to see how you feel, especially over a long period of time.

A picnic

We asked you to describe a perfect picnic – thank you to everyone who **wrote in**! Here are some of your letters.

My husband and I celebrate our wedding anniversary by **going on** a picnic every July. We **make our way to** the coast, stopping to **pick up** some food and drinks on the way. We love being **on our own** together, **off the beaten track**, and we just sit and chat and watch the ocean. After we've eaten, we walk along the coast and only **turn back** when the sun **goes down**. It's a magical day.

Ginny and Raoul

To celebrate Mum's birthday, we went on a picnic in a country park near here. We got there before Mum and Dad, and **took advantage of** the picnic tables provided down by the river. My brother had **invested in** a special picnic basket, and organized all the food. He and I **set** it all **up**, but other family members **pitched in**, and even the kids helped to **clear up** at the end. Mum was delighted, and best of all, the mosquitoes **stayed away** ▼.

Julia

write in write to an organization to ask about sth, tell a story, or express an opinion.
go on sth go somewhere to do a particular activity: *go on a picnic, go on a tour.*
make your way (to somewhere) go to a particular place, especially over some distance or taking some time.
pick sth up INF buy sth.
(all) on your own alone; with no one else.
off the beaten track far away from other people, houses, etc.
turn back turn round and return the way you came.
go down when the sun or moon goes down, it goes below the horizon.
take advantage of sth make use of an opportunity; use sth well.
invest in sth buy sth that is expensive but that you will use a lot or enjoy having.
set sth up prepare equipment, furniture, etc. that will be needed for an activity.
pitch in INF join other people and help with an activity.
clear (sth) up make a place clean and tidy.

WORD FOCUS

There are several phrasal verbs with **stay**.
stay away not come near somebody or something (see text).
stay behind remain somewhere when other people have left: *We stayed behind to help tidy up.*
stay over sleep as a guest in somebody's home for a night: *I stayed over at Tom's.*

A surprise party

'Mum and Dad's fortieth wedding anniversary was **coming up**, and my brother Joe and I wanted to **throw a party** for them. In the end, however, we decided to take them out for lunch with friends and family, but we all agreed to **keep** it **from** them till the last minute. Joe said he would **see to** the restaurant arrangements, and I **took charge of** inviting family and close friends. I was worried that Mum would **get wind of** ▼ the party because Aunty Ann loves gossiping – she **can't help herself** – but fortunately, she didn't **let on**.

On the day of the lunch, we told Mum and Dad that we were taking them out. Mum **got dressed up**, but it didn't **occur to** them that we'd organized anything special.

We **drew up** outside the restaurant, and suddenly Dad spotted Uncle Ron looking very smart. It began to **dawn on** him that this was no ordinary lunch. We went into the dining room and fifty of their relatives and best friends were there, cheering and smiling. Mum looked shocked and then **burst into tears**; Dad just **burst out laughing**. At the end of the meal, someone **yelled out**, 'Speech!', but Dad just smiled and **took no notice**. I know they'll remember the day for the rest of their lives.'

come up USUALLY CONTINUOUS be going to happen very soon.
throw a party organize a party, particularly in your own home.
keep sth from sb avoid telling sb sth.
see to sth deal with sth; take responsibility for sth. SYN take charge of sth.
can't help yourself if you can't help yourself, you can't stop yourself doing sth.
let on tell sb sth, especially sth that is intended to be a secret.
get dressed up wear clothes that are more formal than those you usually wear. (Also dress up.)
occur to sb if sth occurs to you, you suddenly start to think about it.
draw up (of a vehicle) arrive at a place and stop.
dawn on sb if sth dawns on you, you suddenly realize it for the first time.
burst into tears suddenly start to cry.
burst out laughing suddenly start laughing.
yell (sth) out shout sth loudly.
take (no) notice (of sth/sb) (not) pay attention to sth; (not) listen to sth/sb.

WORD FOCUS

If somebody **gets wind of sth** INF, they find out something that is secret or private. This may be because someone else has **spilled the beans** INF, = tell someone something that should be kept secret.

A family meal

ZOE How did your family lunch go?

JAN Well, … these things usually go OK if you **think ahead**, but **to be honest**, it was a bit chaotic. **First of all**, my neighbour, Maria, **popped over** in the morning for a coffee and a chat, and that **held** me **up**, so by midday I'd really **got behind with** the preparation. And after that I was **rushing about** like a lunatic trying to get things organized.

ZOE Oh, dear.

JAN Yes, and the other thing was, I hadn't **bargained on** the change in the weather. We'd planned to have a barbecue because it's been so warm lately, but by lunchtime, it was **pouring with rain,** so in the end we all had to **squeeze into** the kitchen, and I did everything on the cooker.

ZOE Oh, **what a shame** ▼.

JAN Well, actually, it was OK. But then this annoyed me: afterwards, all the women helped **wash up** and **tidy** everything **away**, but the men just **stood around**, **chatting away** as usual.

ZOE Well, that's fairly typical, isn't it!

think ahead think about a future event or situation and plan for it.
to be honest used to tell sb what you really think.
first of all used to introduce the first of several things you are going to say.
pop over/round INF go somewhere quickly or for a short time.
hold sb/sth up delay sb/sth.
get behind (with sth) if you have got behind with a job, you have not done as much of it as you should have by a particular time.
rush about/around try to do a lot of things or go to a lot of places in a short time.
bargain on sth USUALLY NEGATIVE expect sth to happen and be prepared for it.
pour with rain rain very heavily.
squeeze into sth manage to get into a small space. (Also squeeze sb/sth into sth.)
wash up wash plates, glasses, knives, etc.
tidy sth away put things in the place where they should be, e.g. in a drawer, especially so that they cannot be seen.
stand around stand somewhere and do nothing very useful.
chat (away) talk in a relaxed, friendly way.

WORD FOCUS

What a shame is used when you feel sad or disappointed about something. SYN **what a pity**. If you are sorry that something has happened to someone, you can also say **bad luck / hard luck**.

A wedding

I was looking at our wedding photos yesterday, and all these **memories came flooding back**. Ollie and I agreed to get married in the summer of 1990, but I had a difficult time trying to **pin** him **down** to a wedding date! Eventually we **settled on** ▼ July 1st, and started to plan for **the big day**.

Secretly, I wanted a big wedding, but our families had very little money, so we **settled for** ▼ a simple ceremony with just family and close friends, and we had to **do without** a honeymoon. Dad **treated** everyone **to** lunch at a local hotel, and Ollie's friend Dan suggested we had a disco in the garden at home afterwards. I did wonder what would happen if it rained, but I **went along with** it, and **in the event**, it was a glorious, warm evening, and everything **went off without a hitch**.

During the meal, Ollie **got up** and made a lovely speech: it **reduced me to tears**, but it was the best day of my life. We **drank a toast to** a long and happy marriage, and that is what we have had. I wouldn't **swap places with** anyone.

flood back if memories come flooding back, you suddenly remember them very clearly.

pin sb down force sb to make a decision about sth or say what they intend to do.

a/the big day a very important day, e.g. a wedding day.

do without sth manage without sth.

treat sb to sth pay for or do sth special for sb that you know they will like.

go along with sth agree with a plan or decision that sb else has made.

in the event when the situation actually happens.

go off (of an organized event) happen in a particular way. If sth goes off without a hitch, it happens without any problems.

get up stand after sitting, lying, etc. SYN stand up.

reduce sb to tears/silence, etc. make sb cry, be silent, etc.

drink (a toast) to sb/sth wish sb happiness, success with sth, etc. by raising your glasses and drinking from them.

swap places with sb exchange your place or situation for that of sb else.

WORD FOCUS

If you **settle on** something, you choose or make a decision about something after thinking about it.
If you **settle for** something, you accept it, even though it is not the best solution, or not what you would really like.

Rock concerts

How was the last rock concert you went to?

MAL Brilliant! The **warm-up** band **went down** really **well** ▼, so by the time Coldplay **came on**, the atmosphere was electric and we knew we **were in for** a great night. Chris Martin was superb and the band **backed** him **up** really well. We were all **singing along** – a wonderful night. I couldn't have **enjoyed myself** more.

ARI Everyone **went crazy** when Strings' entry was announced, but we all got a bit restless when the band spent so long **testing out** their equipment. People started whistling and **calling out**, but after a couple of songs, they **won** the crowd **over** with the quality of their performance.

LOUELLA It's a strange experience, being at a big concert – it certainly was at the last one I went to. You're all **packed in like sardines**, and the noise is deafening – people are **screaming their heads off**. Then suddenly the crowd starts pushing to get nearer the stage and you're **fighting for breath**. Sometimes people **pass out** in the crush; it's awful. But you're **living in the moment** and it's the most exciting thing you can imagine.

warm-up a warm-up performer prepares the audience for the main show by singing, telling jokes, etc.
come on (of a performer) walk onto a stage.
be in for sth INF be going to experience sth soon.
back sb up give support to sb. (In this case, the musicians back up the main singer.)
sing along (to sth) sing with sb else who is already singing.
enjoy yourself get pleasure from an event or experience.
go crazy if an audience or group of people go crazy, they become very excited.
test sth (out) try using sth to see if it is working correctly or is satisfactory.
call out say or shout sth loudly.
win sb over get sb's support, especially when they were against you before.
packed in like sardines crowded very tightly together in a small space.
scream your head off shout very loudly.
fight for breath have difficulty breathing.
pass out suddenly become unconscious, for example because you are too hot.
live in/for the moment enjoy the present time and not worry about the future.

WORD FOCUS

If a performance **goes down well**, the audience responds enthusiastically and it is a success. (Also **go down a storm/a bomb** INF.) OPP **go down badly**.

A nasty row

'IT ALL STARTED quite quietly. I was standing at the bus stop. A woman behind me was **giving** her daughter **a telling-off** for being lazy. The girl tried to **laugh it off**, but the mother just **went on and on about** how the girl **took** her mother **for granted** and **never lifted a finger** around the house. Finally the daughter just exploded. She started shouting at her mother, and for one awful moment I thought she was going to **go for** ▼ her, so I decided to **step in**. Wow! What a mistake that was. Both women immediately **turned on** ▼ me. The mother told me to **mind my own business**, and the daughter just shouted, '**Clear off**'.

By this stage quite a few people were **looking on**, and I was hoping one of them would **back me up**. But no one did, so I just **walked away**. Further down the road I looked back and they were still **having a go at** each other.'

give sb a telling-off speak angrily to sb, especially a child, because they have done sth wrong. (Also tell sb off.)
laugh sth off joke about sth in order to suggest that it is not serious or important.
go on (and on) about sth/sb talk about sth/sb for a long time, especially in a complaining and boring way.
take sb for granted be so accustomed to sb that you do not appreciate them or show that you are grateful to them.
not lift a finger (to do sth) INF do nothing to help sb.
step in become involved in an argument, especially to stop any trouble.
mind your own business INF stop asking questions and getting involved in other people's lives.
clear off! used to tell sb rudely to go away.
look on watch an activity or event without becoming involved. A person who does this is an onlooker.
back sb up provide support for sb.
walk away leave a place, situation or person.
have a go at sb INF attack or criticize sb.

WORD FOCUS

If you **go for sb**, you attack them physically. If you **turn on sb**, you suddenly attack them verbally or physically.

Riots

The London Riots

THERE HAD been unrest **leading up to** the riots in London in August 2011. The fatal police shooting of 29-year-old Mark Duggan **sparked off** protests, and violence **broke out** when 120 people marched on Tottenham Police Station. Cars **were set on fire**, shops were looted, and a man who was trying to film the events **was beaten up** by rioters. The following day the trouble **spilled over** into other districts, and on the Monday, gangs of youths **wreaked havoc** in many parts of the capital, **burning down** buildings and looting from shops. It was thought that gangleaders were able to organize the riots using their mobile phones.

Initially, the police **came under fire** for their slow response to the events, but by Tuesday morning they were on the streets **in force**, and the trouble had **died down ▼**. **In the wake of** the violence, the prime minister promised that no one would **get away with** robbery and thuggery, and following eyewitness reports and examination of the CCTV footage, the police arrested over 2,000 people. ■

lead up to sth if a problem or series of actions lead up to an important event, they come before it or cause it.
spark sth (off) cause sth to start or develop, especially suddenly.
break out (of a fire, fight or war) begin.
set sth on fire/set fire to sth make sth start burning.
beat sb up hit or kick sb hard, many times.
spill over increase and then affect other areas.
wreak havoc cause very great harm or damage.
burn down/burn sth down be destroyed or destroy sth by fire.
come under fire be attacked or criticized.
in force in large numbers.
in the wake of sth happening after an event or as a result of it.
get away with sth escape punishment after doing sth wrong.

WORD FOCUS

If something **dies down** (usually a fire, noise or trouble), it becomes gradually less strong, loud, unpleasant, etc.
If something **dies away** (usually a sound or noise), it becomes gradually quieter and weaker and then stops: *The sound of footsteps gradually died away.*
If something **dies out** (usually a species), it stops existing: *Tigers are dying out in this part of Africa.*

Storms and flooding

Fresh storms bring chaos

Following gale-force winds that battered homes at the weekend, people along the east coast are now having to **deal with** widespread flooding after 80 mm of rain fell in less than 24 hours. Some residents have **been driven out of** their homes, and the village of Cashford **was** almost **cut off** after a bridge over the River Tane **was swept away**.

Despite warnings, some residents **were** still **caught unawares**, and are only now **coming to terms with** the scale of the devastation. "It's already the worst **in living memory**," said one homeowner. "Water **came in** ▼ during the night, and the ground floor is now completely flooded." And there could be worse to come. Forecasters say the area will have to **contend with** more **downpours** this evening, so many homes are still **at risk from** flooding. It is thought the rain may not **ease off** until later tomorrow.

deal with sth take action to do sth, especially to solve a problem.
drive sb out (of sth) make sb go away or leave a particular place.
cut sth/sb off (from sth) OFTEN PASSIVE make a place difficult to enter, leave or communicate with.
sweep sth away OFTEN PASSIVE (of floods, a tornado, etc.) completely destroy sth.
catch sb unawares happen in a way that sb was not expecting and not prepared for.
come to terms with sth gradually accept a difficult or unpleasant situation.
in living memory during the time that anyone still alive can remember.
contend with sth/sb have to deal with a difficult situation or person.
downpour a large amount of heavy rain. pour down v.
at risk (from/of sth) in a situation in which sth unpleasant or harmful may happen.
ease off become less strong, unpleasant, etc.: *The pain should ease off soon.*

WORD FOCUS

Come in has many meanings. These are three of the most common.
1 enter a room or building (see text).
2 arrive somewhere: *When does his train come in?*
3 be received: *Reports are coming in of further flooding.*

A fight in a fish shop

'I was standing in a queue in my local fish and chip shop last week when four teenage boys **came in**. One of them **was** very **full of himself**, and tried to **show off** to his mates by **pushing in** at the front of the queue. He probably thought that nobody would challenge him, but he was mistaken. The man in front of me **took exception to** his behaviour and told him to get to the back.

The next thing I knew, a fight had **broken out.** One of the boys **threw a punch**, the man momentarily **lost his balance**, and the other three boys jumped on him and tried to **pin** him **down** on the floor. An elderly couple **stood back** and **looked on** in horror while I rang the police. Fortunately, the man working in the fish and chip shop reacted very swiftly to the trouble – perhaps he was used to it. **Quick as a flash**, he produced a fire extinguisher and **turned** it **on** the boys. It must've come as quite a shock to them, because the fight **broke up** almost immediately and the boys **ran away**.

I'd rather lost my appetite by then, so I left. I heard later that the man needed stitches to his face. I don't know if they ever **caught up with** the boys responsible.'

come in enter a room, building, etc.
be full of yourself INF, DISAPPROVING behave in a proud, unpleasant way, showing little thought for other people.
show off INF, DISAPPROVING behave in a way that is intended to attract people's attention and make people admire you.
push in stand in front of people in a queue who have been waiting longer than you.
take exception to sth be angry about sth and object to it strongly.
the next thing I knew used to say that sth happened very quickly and unexpectedly.
break out (of a fight, war or fire) start suddenly.
throw a punch hit sb with your fist (= closed hand).
lose your balance suddenly fall or almost fall.
pin sb down hold sb firmly on the ground so that they cannot move.
stand back move back from sth that is happening.
look on watch an activity or event without taking part in it. onlooker N.
quick as a flash very quickly. SYN like a flash.
turn sth on sb/sth direct sth such as a water hose or a gun at sb or sth.
break up (of a fight) stop.
run away escape by running out of a place.
catch up with sb find and arrest sb who has committed a crime.

Mountain rescue

WHEN Carol Stephens and Sian Crane **set off** for a day's hiking, the weather was fine. By mid morning, however, it was already **closing in**, and by lunchtime it was foggy, the rain was **coming down**, and it was difficult to see where they were going. They decided to **start back** and tried to **figure out** the best route, but they **lost their bearings.** In the confusion, Sian tripped on the edge of the mountainside and fell nearly twenty feet. She landed on a ledge but was unconscious. Carol immediately **called out** the mountain rescue team, who were **on the spot** within half an hour. By this time, Sian had **come to** and was **complaining of** ▼ a terrible pain in her leg. The rescue crew were able to reach her, but had to call for helicopter **backup** to get her off the ledge. She was rushed to hospital where doctors **attended to** her leg, which was broken in two places.

Carol said it hadn't **dawned on** them that they were taking a risk with the weather. "One thing's for sure, we'll **think twice about** doing anything like that again," she said.

set off start a journey, especially a long journey.

close in if the weather is closing in, dark clouds and stormy conditions are approaching.

come down (of rain, snow, etc.) fall.

start back begin to return somewhere.

figure sth out think about a problem or situation until you find the answer or understand it. SYN work sth out.

lose your bearings become lost or confused.

call sb out ask sb to come, especially to an emergency.

on the spot at the actual place where sth is happening.

come to become conscious again. SYN come around/round.

backup extra support that can be used if necessary. back sb up v.

attend to sb/sth take care of sb/sth; deal with sb/sth.

dawn on sb if sth dawns on you, you understand it or realize it is true for the first time.

think twice about sth/doing sth consider carefully whether sth you are planning to do is a good idea.

WORD FOCUS

If somebody **complains of sth**, they say that they feel sick or are in some pain (see text). This verb is not used in the first person in the present tense: ~~I'm complaining of pain.~~

15.1 STUDY

Memories of school

Think back to your schooldays and answer the questionnaire!

- Which subjects did you **do well at**?
- Did you find it hard to **keep up with** other students in the class, or certain subjects?
- Did you have to **learn** a lot of things **by heart**, e.g. in history or science?
- Were you good at **getting down to** your homework once you got home?
- If you were away from school because you were ill, did you have to **catch up on** work when you went back?
- Did your teachers ever **mark** you **down** for making spelling mistakes?
- Did you ever **get told off** ▼ for being late?
- Did you ever **doze off** in a lesson?
- Did you ever **play truant**?
- Did your teachers ever tell you to **pull your socks up**?
- Did your teachers ever **keep** you **in** after school to do extra work?
- **Was** anyone ever **thrown out** of your school for bad behaviour?
- How did you feel when you **broke up** at the end of term?

think back (to sth) think about sth that happened in the past.
do well (at sth) be successful in sth. OPP do badly (at sth).
keep up (with sb/sth) make progress in sth at the same speed as other people or at the right level.
learn sth by heart study sth so that it is stored in your memory.
get down to sth start doing sth seriously and with effort.
catch up on sth spend extra time doing sth that should have been done before.
mark sb down reduce the mark or grade given to sb in a written piece of work or an exam.
doze off go to sleep, especially during the day.
play truant stay away from school without permission.
pull your socks up INF try to improve your work, behaviour, etc.
keep sb in make sb stay indoors or in a particular place, often in school as a punishment.
throw sb out force sb to leave a place.
break up begin the holidays when school finishes at the end of term.

WORD FOCUS

If you **tell sb off**, you speak angrily to them for doing something wrong. It is often used in the passive: *I got told off for breaking a window.* You also **give sb a telling-off** N.

Classroom actions

copy it down (= write exactly what sb has written or said)

cross it out

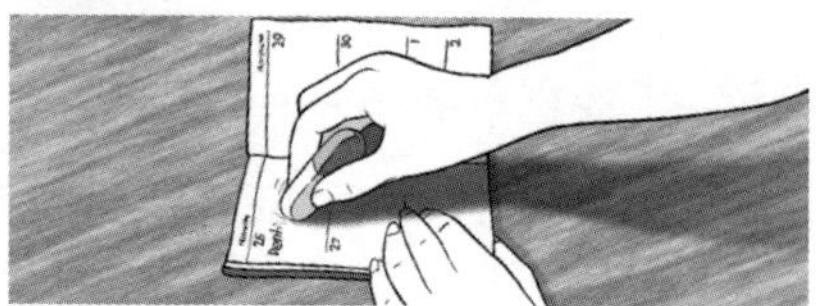

rub it out

1 I live _in_ France.
2 Look ____ of the window.
3 She comes _from_ Germany.

leave it out (= don't do number 2)

NAME Adriano Clerici
DATE OF BIRTH 16.4.1992
ADDRESS

fill it in (= complete it)

print it out

hand it in (= give sth to your teacher or someone in authority)

hand it out (= give sth to different people in a group)

put it away

turn it over

What teachers say

If you don't know the meaning of a word, **look** it **up** in a dictionary or ask me to explain it to you.

OK, everyone, look at the **handout**, and Jaime, could you **read out** the opening lines of the text, please?

I'm sorry you've been ill, Yuki, but these handouts will help you to **catch up with** the rest of the class.

OK, let's **clear this up, once and for all**! The past tense of 'spell' can be either 'spelled' or 'spelt'.

OK, everyone, **finish off** this exercise tonight, and we'll **go through** it tomorrow. Now, let's **move on to** something else …

When you've done your essay **in rough**, you'll need to give me a typed version.

Work with your partner and **take it in turns** to test each other on the vocabulary.

Don't worry about that bit of grammar; we'll **come back to** it later.

Pasha, could you and Katya **swap places**, please? Thank you.

Right, everyone, it's nearly 6.00. Let's **call it a day**, shall we?

look sth up find information by looking in a dictionary, reference book, etc.
handout a piece of paper containing information, a text, exercises, etc. given to students in a class. hand sth out v.
read sth out read sth aloud so that other people can hear you.
catch up with sb reach the same level or standard as sb who is more advanced.
clear sth up solve a problem or explain sth that sb has not understood.
once and for all completely and finally.
finish sth off do the last part of sth so that it is complete.
go through sth examine sth in detail.
move on to sth stop talking about or doing one thing and start talking about or doing a different thing.
in rough if you write sth in rough, you make a first version of it, and you will improve it later.
take it in turns if people take it in turns to do sth, they do it one after another so that everyone has the opportunity to do it. SYN take turns at sth.
come back to sth return to sth that you were discussing, studying, etc. earlier.
swap places exchange seats or positions with sb.
call it a day INF decide to stop what you are doing (often work).

Exam revision tips

How to get through exams

- The most important thing is to **draw up** a timetable for revision, and then **stick to** it.

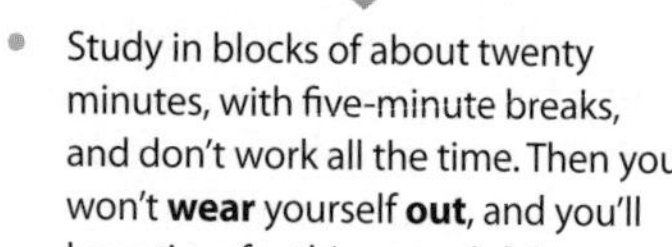

- Study in blocks of about twenty minutes, with five-minute breaks, and don't work all the time. Then you won't **wear** yourself **out**, and you'll have time for things to **sink in**.

- Just **flicking through** ▼ your books and notes isn't very helpful. **Jot down** some notes on what you're reading, and **make up** quizzes or memory aids, such as cards with key words on. Even **copying** something **out** is more effective than just reading.

- **Work your way through** all the past papers you can **get your hands on**. Practise answering questions **against the clock**. It's also helpful to try to **work out** which topics tend to **come up** regularly, and focus on them.

- **Look after yourself**! The night before the exam, don't **stay up** all night; try to get a good night's sleep. And on the actual day, eat something that will **keep you going** through the exam, such as eggs or pasta.

draw sth up prepare a plan, schedule, programme, etc.
stick to sth continue to do sth that you decided or promised to do.
wear sb out make sb feel very tired.
sink in become completely understood.
jot sth down write sth quickly.
make sth up invent sth.
copy sth out write sth again, exactly as it has been written.
work your way through sth do or study one thing after another, missing nothing out.
get your hands on sth INF succeed in getting sth.
against the clock trying very hard to finish sth before a particular time.
work sth out resolve or decide sth by thinking about it carefully.
come up if a topic comes up in an exam, it appears in the exam.
look after sb take care of sb.
stay up delay going to bed.
keep sb going if sth to eat keeps you going, it stops you feeling hungry and gives you enough energy to do sth.

WORD FOCUS

If you **flick through** a book, you turn the pages quickly without reading them carefully (see text).
If you **flick through** TV channels, you change them quickly to see what programmes are on.

Exam results

Student Exam Forum

How did your exams go?

CARRIE I thought my exams had gone badly, and I **was in a terrible state** before the results **came out**. I was right about the physics exam – I **messed** that **up** – but I **sailed through** the other subjects and got three 'As'!

LYALL I knew I **didn't stand a chance of** passing the history exam. I **missed out** a couple of questions, and then I couldn't **come up with** any ideas for the essay. My mind just **went blank**.

LUCIA I passed the exams **with flying colours**, but then I still had to **get through** an interview for medical school. I did really badly and I didn't **get in**. It was so disappointing.

JASON I did well in my course work, and that **counted towards** my final results. I just **scraped through** the exams, but still got a university place.

RANI My first-year results were poor, so I decided that law **was not for** me. I **gave** it **up** and did history instead.

be in a bad/terrible state INF be very anxious or upset about sth.
come out become known.
mess sth up make a mistake and do sth badly.
sail through sth succeed very easily in a test, exam or course.
stand a chance of doing sth USUALLY NEGATIVE if you don't stand a chance of doing sth, it is not possible that you will succeed in doing it.
miss sth out not do sth or include sth.
come up with sth find or produce an answer, idea, etc.
go blank if your mind goes blank, you cannot remember sth, especially the answer to a question.
with flying colours if you pass sth with flying colours, you are very successful.
get through sth be successful in a test, an interview, etc.
get in/get into sth be accepted to study at a school, university, etc.
count towards sth be included as part of sth you hope to achieve in the future.
scrape through (sth) succeed in doing sth such as passing an exam, but doing it with difficulty or not doing it well.
not be for sb INF if sth is not for you, it is not the kind of thing that you like or that is suitable for you.
give sth up stop doing sth that you were trying hard to do.

Why learn a language?

Language learning can **open up** a wide range of opportunities for you **in terms of** work, pleasure and cultural enrichment.

- In business, a foreign language can help you **build up** an awareness of cultural differences and **smooth the path for** trade negotiations.
- On holiday abroad, even if you can only **get by** in the language, your stay will be more enjoyable. Spend a little time **brushing up on** your school Spanish before you go to Spain, and you will have the satisfaction of talking to someone in another language. Most people appreciate that you have made the effort to speak their language.
- If you live abroad, knowledge of the native tongue will enable you to **play a** greater **part in** the community, and in some cases **act as** an ambassador, trying to **bridge the gap between** the cultures.
- At home, too, knowledge of a language can make you **stand out** in university applications. Furthermore, once you've learnt one foreign language, you will know how to **go about** learning another, and may find it easier to **pick it up** ▼.

open sth up create new possibilities.
in terms of sth used to show what aspect of a subject you are talking about.
build sth up gradually create or develop sth.
smooth the path/way (for sth) remove problems so that sth can develop easily.
get by if you can get by in a language, you know just enough of it to be able to do what you need to do.
brush up on sth / brush sth up practise and improve your knowledge of and skills in sth that you learned in the past.
play a part in sth be involved in sth.
act as sth/sb do a particular job, or play a particular role.
bridge the gap between A and B reduce or get rid of the differences between two things or two groups of people.
stand out (from sb/sth) be easy to notice or see because of being different: *stand out in a crowd.*
go about doing sth start dealing with a situation, a job, etc. in a particular way.

WORD FOCUS

Pick sth up has many meanings. Here are three of the most common.
1 learn a new skill easily or by chance, without working hard at it (see text).
2 lift something up from a surface: *I picked up all the toys that were on the floor.*
3 collect something from a place: *I'll pick your jacket up at the cleaners.*

Getting a job

Top tips for job applications

When you are applying for a job, remember these useful tips:

- Do some research on the company that you are interested in. A good understanding of their business will make you **stand out from** other candidates, and make you appear organized and thorough.
- Write a CV which **makes a** good **impression** by presenting it in a very professional way. **Flag up** your positive characteristics, but try not to seem as if you are boasting. It is essential to **point out** how your skills **relate to** the particular job that you are applying for. Always ask someone you can **rely on** to **look over** your letter and CV, and suggest some improvements.
- Prepare for the interview if you are offered one. **Make sure** you know your way there, and of course, **show up** ▼ on time. Deciding what to wear **depends on** the sort of job you**'re after**, so think about it carefully.
- The interview is an opportunity for you and the potential employer to **find out** more about each other. Here are some simple tips: don't sit down until you're invited to; **speak up** – don't mumble; keep to the facts; and emphasize the ways in which you would **be up to** the job.

stand out (from sb/sth) be easy to see or notice because of being different.
make an impression (on sb) make other people notice and admire you.
flag sth up mention sth that you think is important.
point sth out tell sb sth in order to make them notice it.
relate to sth be connected to sth or be about sth.
rely on sb/sth trust sb/sth and have faith in them to do sth for you.
look sth over examine sth to see how good it is.
make sure check sth so that you can be certain about it.
depend on sth be affected or decided by something else.
be after sth be wanting or looking for sth.
find sth out or find out about sb/sth get information about sb/sth by asking, reading, etc.
speak up speak loudly enough to be clearly heard.
be up to sth be good enough for sth.

WORD FOCUS

Show up and **turn up** are informal phrasal verbs meaning 'arrive'. When you **show up** at a place, you are usually expected: *She didn't show up for work.* When you **turn up**, you may or may not be expected: *Don't bother to book a place – just turn up when you want to.*

Job likes and dislikes

What do you like about your job?

JOSH I'm a marketing consultant. Helping my clients **sort out** ▼ their business problems and **get** their message **across** to their customers is very rewarding.

ALEXA I enjoy **dealing with** the public – every day is different.

SAM I feel I'm **making the most of** my skills, and that's satisfying.

MARIA I work for an organization that I **believe in**, which means a lot.

What don't you like about your job?

RONI All I do is **fill out** forms. I'm **bored to tears** most of the time.

DEV I **thrive on** challenge, and it's just not there. All I do is **go over** the same tasks **again and again**.

LOUELLA **Getting bogged down in** paperwork – that's the worst bit.

ENRICO My boss has never really made clear what my role is. I spend ages trying to **figure out** what I**'m supposed to** be doing.

RUDY In meetings, my boss **pulls** me **to pieces** in front of my colleagues. I hate it.

get sth across communicate sth clearly.
deal with sb be involved with sb in a business sense.
make the most of sth use a situation to get the best possible result.
believe in sth feel that a person or an organization is good or right.
fill sth out complete a form by writing information on it. SYN fill sth in.
bored to tears extremely bored. SYNS bored stiff, bored to death.
thrive on sth enjoy sth such as hard work or a difficult task, and be stimulated by it.
go over sth study or check the details of sth.
again and again many times.
get/be bogged down (in sth) become so involved with the details of sth that you cannot make progress.
figure sth out think about a problem or situation until you find the answer or understand it. SYN work sth out.
be supposed to do sth be expected to do sth by sb in authority or because of rules.
pull sb to pieces INF criticize sb or their work very severely.

WORD FOCUS

If you **sort** a problem **out**, you deal with it successfully. If something **sorts itself out**, it stops being a problem and no one has to do anything about it.

Better job performance

- Make a list of things to **get through** that day – and **work on** them in order of priority. This will help you to **filter out** unnecessary or unimportant tasks.
- Work on the tasks **one at a time**. Don't **go on to** a new task before you have finished the previous one.
- If you're working on a big task, **break** it **down** into smaller tasks; this will give you more sense of achievement.
- Don't **be put off** ▼ by colleagues who want to stop and chat. Tell them politely that you're too busy to talk.
- Check your email inbox at the start of the day and answer anything important. After that, **set aside** specific times to check and reply to emails.
- Reduce paperwork by storing important information on your computer.
- Don't **put off doing** ▼ things because you don't like them. It may help to **get** them **out of the way** early in the day.
- **Tidy up** your desk regularly. If your things are **all over the place**, you won't be able to work efficiently.
- Finally, if you**'re snowed under** at work, don't be afraid to ask for help. ■

get through sth finish dealing with a series of tasks or a piece of work.

work on sth spend time producing or improving sth.

filter sth out remove sth that you do not want from a larger number of things.

one at a time separately and in order. SYN one by one.

go on to (do) sth do sth after doing sth else.

break sth down divide sth into different parts to make it easier to do or deal with.

set sth aside if you set aside time or money, you save it in order to use it later for a particular purpose.

get sth out of the way finish doing sth, especially sth difficult or unpleasant.

tidy sth up make a room, desk, etc. look better by putting things in the correct place.

all over the place not neat or tidy; not well organized.

be snowed under (with sth) have more work than you are able to deal with.

WORD FOCUS

If someone **puts you off**, they disturb you while you are trying to concentrate (see text).
If you **put sth off** or **put off doing sth**, you delay doing something because you don't want to do it (see text), or because you decide to do it at a later time.

Colleagues

Tell us about your colleagues!

SEAN My co-worker, Janine, is great. I can **turn to** her if I have a problem or if there's something that I need to **talk over**. She can **get along with** ▼ anyone! I feel she trusts me, and she always **backs** me **up** in meetings. I know her so well now that really I **look on** her **as** a friend.

TIM **I've got a lot of time for** our head of department, Clive. He **brings out the best in** everyone. We all **look up to** him, but he's basically a very modest guy.

SAM Leon's great; you know he'll **pull out all the stops** to finish the work on time and to a high standard. And he **comes up with** all the best ideas in meetings.

TIA I can't stand Mr Harrison. He's always **showing off** in front of the boss. And he's so patronising – he just **talks down to** me all the time.

WILLY Dan's nice, but I don't think he**'s cut out to be** a salesman. I think he should change his career path.

turn to sb/sth go to sb/sth for help, advice, etc.

talk sth over (with sb) discuss sth in detail, especially in order to make a decision or reach an agreement.

back sb up support sb by telling other people you agree with that person.

look on sb as sth/sb think of sb in a particular way.

have (got) a lot of time for sb/sth INF like and be interested in sb/sth.

bring out the best/worst in sb make sb show their best/worst qualities.

look up to sb admire and respect sb. OPP look down on sb.

pull out (all) the stops INF make the greatest effort possible to achieve sth.

come up with sth find or produce an answer, a new idea, money, etc.

show off INF, DISAPPROVING try to impress other people by talking about your abilities, possessions, etc. show-off N.

talk down to sb speak to sb as if they are not as clever or important as you.

be cut out for sth / to be sth INF, USUALLY NEGATIVE have all the qualities or abilities needed for sth.

WORD FOCUS

If you **get along with sb**, you have a good relationship with them (see text). Two people can **get along**: *How do you and Jack get along?* SYN **get on (with sb)**.

Losing your job

I used to be the receptionist in a hotel which had a reputation for excellent food. Then it **was taken over** by a big hotel chain. The manager decided to **hand in his notice**, and the hotel **took on** a new manager who was awful. She **made life** very **difficult for** the head chef, and one day she just **gave him the sack** ▼. She then **brought in** her own chef who was useless, and as a result the number of guests just started **dropping off**.

Eventually, they started **laying** people **off** ▼, and I found myself without a job. It took time for the realization of being unemployed to **sink in**, and for a couple of months I just **sat around**, not doing very much, and **feeling sorry for myself**. I had very little money to **live on** and had started to **run up** debts.

Then, one day, I had a drink with the old chef and colleagues who had also been **made redundant** ▼. We got chatting and someone suggested we work together to **start up** a new restaurant. **It's early days**, but we're all very excited and optimistic about it. ●

take sth over take control of a business, often by buying shares in it. takeover N.

hand in your notice/resignation say officially that you have decided to leave your job.

take sb on start to employ sb.

make life/things difficult for sb cause problems for sb.

bring sb in ask sb to do a particular job.

drop off become fewer or less.

sink in be fully understood or realized.

sit around spend time doing nothing very useful. SYN sit about.

feel sorry for yourself INF, DISAPPROVING feel unhappy about sth, but not try to do anything to improve the situation.

live on sth have a particular amount of money for the basic things you need.

run sth up allow a bill or debt to reach a large total.

start sth up if you start up a business, you create or establish it. SYN set sth up.

it's early days used to say that it is too soon to know if sth will be successful.

WORD FOCUS

If someone **gives you the sack**, they tell you that you can no longer work for them because you have done something wrong. (Also **get the sack**: *He got the sack for constant lateness.*) If you **are laid off**, you have to leave your job because there is not enough work for you. SYN **be made redundant**.

Buying an existing business

Some people **start up** their own business because they create a new product or service; others spot **a gap in the market**; a few have an interest or hobby that they **turn into** a business. Many, however, still follow the well-trodden path of buying an existing business. But you must first consider the advantages and disadvantages of what you are **taking on**.

ADVANTAGES

- The basic work of getting the business **up and running** has already been done.
- It may be easier to **get your hands on** finance.
- There may be regular customers and a regular income that you can **capitalize on** and **build on**.
- A business plan and marketing method should already be **in place**.
- Existing employees should have valuable experience for you to **draw on**.

DISADVANTAGES

- Buying **a going concern** may be very expensive.
- You may have to **put in** ▼ more money **on top of** the purchase price.
- The existing owner may be **selling up** for reasons you are not aware of, and you might find you are **taking over** a business with more problems than you realize.

start sth up if you start up a business, you create or establish it. SYN set sth up.
a gap in the market an opportunity to produce sth that people would like to have, which is not yet available.
turn sth into sth make sth become sth different.
take sth on decide to do sth, or agree to be responsible for sth.
up and running working fully and correctly.
get your hands on sth succeed in getting sth that you want or need.
capitalize on sth gain an extra advantage for yourself from a situation.
build on sth use sth as the basis for more progress.
in place if sth is in place, it exists and is able to be used.
draw on sth use a supply of sth that is available to you.
a going concern a business that makes a profit and is expected to continue to do well.
on top of sth in addition to sth else.
sell up sell your home, business, etc., often because you are retiring or leaving the area.
take sth over take control of sth.

WORD FOCUS

If you **put in** money, you invest it in a business or an account (see text). You can also **put money into sth**: *They put the money into buying an apartment.*

A growing business

WHEN Paul Pritchard opened a pharmacy in a small parade of shops on the outskirts of town, few people thought he would ever **make a go of** it. The shop had formerly **belonged to** a couple selling fruit and vegetables, and before that it had been a hardware shop; both owners had eventually been forced to **close down**. Paul, however, thought differently, and firmly **believed in** what he was doing. **It was touch and go** for several years, but through his energy and enthusiasm he at least managed to **break even**. Then he had **a stroke of luck**. The small doctor's surgery down the road was rebuilt and extended, and two new doctors **were taken on** at the practice. This **had a** dramatic **knock-on effect on** Paul's business, and the number of people coming into the pharmacy almost doubled **at a stroke**. From then on, Paul gradually **built up** the business, and in five years' time, when he retires, he hopes to be able to **pass on** a thriving pharmacy to his nephew, Darren, who is planning to **go into** ▼ the business. ●

make a go of sth INF be successful in sth that is difficult or requires effort.
belong to sb if sth belongs to you, it is yours; you own it.
close down permanently stop operating or doing business.
believe in sth think that an idea or way of doing sth is good or right.
it's touch and go INF used about a situation in which a successful result is possible but not certain.
break even if a business breaks even, it neither makes a profit nor loses money.
a stroke of luck sth lucky that happens to you unexpectedly.
take sb on employ sb.
have a knock-on effect (on sth) start a process which causes sth to happen, and that then causes sth else to happen.
at a stroke with a single action that has an immediate effect.
build sth up develop sth over time.
pass sth on give sth to sb else, especially after having or using it yourself.

WORD FOCUS

Go into sth has several meanings.
1 start to work in a particular industry or area of activity (see text).
2 talk about sth in detail: *The company won't go into their offer in any detail.*
3 (of money, time, effort, etc.) be spent on sth or used for sth: *A large percentage of the budget has gone into marketing.*

A struggling business

In business, things may **go wrong** for many reasons.

MONEY: Some companies underestimate the funding they need; others use all their **start-up** ▼ capital before they have a steady income; some companies obtain funding, then find it **dries up**.

PEOPLE: Poor management often **lets** a company **down**. Bad managers have a tendency to make impulsive decisions without **weighing up** the **pros and cons**. They also seem to attract, employ and retain people who will **hold** them **back**.

COSTS: It is easy for costs to **get out of control** unless someone is **keeping their eye on the ball**.

COMPETITORS: You have to **keep one step ahead of** your competitors, otherwise you risk **falling behind**.

AMBITION: Some companies are over-ambitious. They need to build and grow, but should do so **one step at a time**.

THE MARKET: Some companies fail to adapt to a changing marketplace, e.g. by failing to **keep up with** the latest technology.

LOCATION: Don't be tempted by a cheap lease or low rent: a company in the wrong place will fail.

go wrong if sth goes wrong, it develops badly and causes problems.
dry up if a supply of sth dries up, there is gradually less of it until there is none left.
let sth down have a bad effect on the quality or success of sth.
weigh sth up consider the good and bad aspects of sth in order to reach a decision.
pros and cons (of sth) the advantages and disadvantages of sth.
hold sb/sth back stop the progress and development of sb/sth.
be/get out of control be or become impossible to manage or control.
keep your eye on the ball continue to give your attention to what is most important.
keep/be one step ahead of sb be better prepared for sth or know more about sth than sb else.
fall behind make less progress or be less successful than other people who are doing a similar job or activity.
one/a step at a time slowly and gradually from one stage to the next. SYN step by step.
keep up with sth be aware of the latest developments in an area or activity.

WORD FOCUS

The adjective **start-up** is only used before a noun, and relates to the start of a new business or project: *start-up costs, start-up capital.* **start sth up** v. A **start-up** is a business that is being started.

Going bankrupt

Should you declare bankruptcy?

If you are facing a serious downturn in business and cannot **pay off** your debts, you may feel the best option is to declare bankruptcy and **wind up** the business. The matter is then taken **out of your hands** and **dealt with** ▼ by the courts, so people cannot come to your home demanding money. In many cases the majority of debts **are** also **written off**, which allows you to make **a fresh start** and **set up** a new company if you wish.

However, there are serious disadvantages to declaring bankruptcy. Other people will **take over** the running of your company, and you will probably have to **sell off** some of your assets. Moreover, legal costs can be expensive, and the whole process may be very time-consuming. For this reason, you should always consider whether you can **turn around** the business, for example with a CVA (Company Voluntary Arrangement) in which you arrange to **pay back** your creditors over a period of time. The existing directors remain in control, and the company does not **go out of business**; it is free to continue trading.

pay sth off finish paying money that you owe for sth.

wind sth up close a business. (If you wind down a business, you bring it to an end gradually over a period of time.)

out of your hands if sth is out of your hands, you are no longer responsible for it.

write sth off say officially that an amount of money does not have to be paid: *write off a debt.*

a fresh start a situation in which you start sth again in a completely different way.

set sth up start sth such as a business, organization, etc.

take sth over take control of sth.

sell sth off sell all or part of an industry, a business, or a piece of land.

turn sth around/round cause a business, economy, etc. to stop being unsuccessful and start being successful.

pay sb back give sb the same amount of money that you borrowed from them.

go out of business stop operating as a business because there is no more money or work available. SYN go bust INF.

WORD FOCUS

If you **deal with sth**, you perform a task, or take action to solve a problem (see text). If you **deal with sb** (a particular person or company), it often means you do business with that person or company: *We deal with a lot of small hotels.*

Management buyout

Prevera buyout to go ahead

The management **buyout** ▼ at Prevera Electronics still looks set to **go ahead**. The proposed deal has had to **contend with** various **setbacks** in recent weeks. First, there were rumours that talks between the management and their principal backer, EPC, had **broken down**, with some commentators claiming that EPC were threatening to **pull out** altogether. Then, last week, one of the original management team, Daniel Evans, decided to **back out**. This prompted fears once again that the deal could be **on the verge of** collapse.

However, the spokesman for the management group, Peter York, has been quick to **put** investors' **minds at ease**. In a statement he made last night, he not only reiterated that EPC were fully behind the deal, he also took the slightly unusual step of announcing that the management team were able to **call on** additional sources of income if necessary. He said, 'I believe there was never any danger of this deal **falling through**, and I hope we will be able to **press ahead with** the buyout as quickly as possible'. The City is expecting an announcement early next week.

go ahead happen or proceed.

contend with sth/sb have to deal with a problem or a difficult situation or person.

setback a difficulty or problem that prevents or delays sb/sth. set sb/sth back V.

break down if a relationship or discussion breaks down, it fails and comes to an end. breakdown N.

pull out stop being involved in an activity, event or situation.

back out decide not to do sth that you agreed to do.

on the verge of (doing) sth very near to the moment when sth happens or sb does sth.

put sb's mind at ease do or say sth to make sb stop worrying about sth.

call on sth decide to use sth that sb can offer you.

fall through if a deal or plan falls through, it fails and doesn't happen.

press ahead (with sth) continue doing sth in a determined way and as quickly as possible, despite difficulties.

WORD FOCUS

A **buyout** occurs when the managers of a company take control of it by buying a majority of the shares. **buy sb out** V. A **takeover** is when a company takes control of another company, also by buying a majority of the shares. **take sth over** V.

Company rescue

BARNEY MORTON describes how he rescued an ailing company

When I **took on** the greetings card company, it had been **going downhill** for quite a while, so I **got down to** work **at once.**

The first part of the job was the hardest, but there was no way round it: I had to **lay off** several members of staff who had been with the company for many years.

It also became clear quite quickly that expenditure **was** spiralling **out of control**, so I **brought in** a new accountant to **get to grips with** the financial side of things.

Stock control was another issue. I realized that if we reduced the amount of stock we held at any one time, it would **free up** more money for marketing, which had been badly neglected. That we have now started to do.

Being a very traditional company, it had not embraced modern technology very quickly. For example, the company hadn't created online greeting cards, and **as a consequence** we were **losing out to** some of our closest competitors.

It'll take time, but we've **improved on** last year's performance, and I now feel we can **turn** the company **round**.

take sth on agree to be responsible for sth.

go downhill get worse in quality, health, etc.

get down to sth start to do sth, giving it serious attention.

at once immediately; without delay.

lay sb off stop employing sb because there is not enough work for them to do or money to pay them. SYN make sb redundant.

be/get out of control be or become impossible to manage. OPP be/get under control.

bring sb in start to employ sb who has particular skills.

get to grips with sth begin to understand and deal with sth difficult.

free sth up make available sth such as money, time or space that was going to be used for another purpose.

as a consequence FML used to say that one thing is the result of another. SYN in consequence.

lose out (to sb/sth) INF not get business, etc. that you expected because sb/sth else has taken it.

improve on sth achieve or produce sth that is of a better quality than sth else.

turn sth around/round if a business, economy, etc. turns around, or sb turns it around, it starts to develop successfully after being unsuccessful for a time.

A future prime minister?

DESTINED FOR THE TOP?

SCHOOL AND UNIVERSITY friends of Daniel Curran say that he **takes after** his illustrious father: clever, creative and very ambitious. Those qualities have certainly **been to the fore** in his rapid rise to the top of his party.

Curran did not **set out to be** a politician, but after two years as a barrister, he **turned his back on** a career in law, and chose the Labour Party instead. He became a Member of Parliament when a seat **came up** near his home town of Salford, and he soon **stood out as** one of the up-and-coming MPs of his generation.

Curran then advanced rapidly **under the wing** of former cabinet minister James Brough, and **hit the headlines** when he **stood for** ▼ leader of the party at the very young age of 38. He narrowly lost on that occasion, but got his chance again three years later when James Dingwall decided to **stand down** for personal reasons. This time Curran **swept to victory**, and he could soon **be heading for** the top if, as many now believe, the prime minister is forced to call a general election later this year. ✻

take after sb look or behave like an older member of your family, especially your father or mother.
be to the fore be/become important and noticed by people.
set out to be/do sth begin a job, task, etc. with a particular aim or goal.
turn your back on sth reject sth that you have previously accepted.
come up become available.
stand out (as sth) be noticeably successful and better than others in a particular role.
under sb's wing being looked after by sb who is older or more experienced.
hit/grab/make the headlines be an important item of news on the TV or radio, or in the newspapers.
stand down leave a job or position, especially an important one.
sweep to victory win a contest easily.
be heading for sth if you are heading for sth, it is likely to happen soon.

WORD FOCUS

Stand for sth has different meanings:
1 try to get chosen in an election for a particular position (see text).
2 be an abbreviation or symbol of something: *UN stands for United Nations.*
3 USUALLY NEGATIVE (not) be willing to accept something that somebody else does: *Some workers are lazy, and the new boss won't stand for that.*

Political sound bites

A *sound bite* is a short comment, often made by a politician and usually taken from a longer speech. It is repeated because it is considered to be especially interesting or effective. The following sound bites are often used by politicians of all parties in **the run-up to** an election.

I am here to **focus on** the issues.

We will **stand up to** the banks and big business.

We won't **give in to** terrorism.

I'm here to **make a difference**.

We must **look to** the future now, and **leave** the past **behind**.

We still **have a long way to go**, but together, we can **make it**.

Our party **stands for** family values.

It's no good the opposition trying to deceive the people; they won't **fall for** it.

There's no **hidden agenda** in our party.

We've **looked at** the opposition's economic policy, and I can tell you now that the figures don't **add up**.

Remember, it's our children's future that is **at stake**.

the run-up to sth the period of time just before an important event.

focus on sth pay particular attention to sth.

stand up to sb/sth refuse to accept bad treatment from a person or organization.

give in (to sth/sb) accept that you have lost in a game, fight, competition, etc.; surrender.

make a difference have an important effect on sth, especially a good effect.

look to sth consider sth and think how to make it better.

leave sth behind stop being involved with a person, place or situation.

have a long way to go need to make a lot more progress before you achieve or complete sth.

make it be successful in a particular activity, especially a career.

stand for sth if sb stands for a particular principle, they believe it is important.

it's no good doing sth = it's not useful or effective to do sth.

fall for sth INF be tricked and deceived into believing that sth is true.

hidden agenda a secret reason for doing sth because you will get an advantage from it.

look at sth examine sth carefully.

add up USUALLY NEGATIVE if a set of facts do not add up, you do not believe they are correct.

at stake likely to be lost or damaged if sth fails.

Election night

"Well, here in Stroud, they've been busily **counting up** the votes for hours, and we're now just minutes away from finding out the result. The parties have been **running neck and neck** throughout the campaign, and **judging by** the faces of the two main rivals, it is still **too close to call**. Many Conservative voters had been hoping that Martin Piper would be able to **build on** the narrow majority he secured at the last election. But when he **came out** strongly **in favour of** the government's proposed pay freeze, some of his supporters feared it may have damaged his chances. His opponents have certainly been quick to **capitalize on** this, and now sense they could be **on the verge of** victory. Much, though, could **hinge on** the **turnout**. We are hearing it is quite low, so this might just **tip the balance in** Piper's **favour**.

I can now see a number of people **crowding around** Martin Horwood, the returning officer, so I think we'**re about to** get the result. Yes, **here we go** . . ."

count (up) sth calculate the total number of things in a group (in this case, votes).
neck and neck (with sb) if you are running neck and neck with sb, you are level with them in a race, competition, etc.
judging by/from sth used to give your reason why you think sth is true.
too close to call if the result of a competition or election is too close to call, it is impossible to know for certain who the winner will be.
build on sth use sth as a basis for further progress.
come out in favour of sth/against sth say publicly that you agree or disagree with sth.
capitalize on sth get an advantage for yourself from a situation.
on the verge of sth very near the moment when sth happens or sb does sth.
hinge on/upon sth (of a result, action, etc.) depend on sth.
turnout the number of people who vote in a particular election.
tip the balance affect the result of sth in one way rather than another.
in sb's favour if sth is in sb's favour, it gives them an advantage or helps them.
crowd around/round (sb/sth) stand together in large numbers around sb/sth.
be about to do sth be going to do sth very soon.
here we go INF said when sth is starting to happen.

Opinions about politicians

What's your opinion of politicians?

Well, **for my money**, they're a waste of time – the whole lot of them.

Politicians often **get a bad press**, but I'm sure they're **doing their best**.

I don't like the way that politicians **talk down to** people. They often treat us as if we're stupid.

I wish politicians would tell us what they really think. It **gets on my nerves** the way they just **toe the party line** all the time.

I think most of them genuinely **believe in** what they're doing, and I respect that.

In my opinion, a few of them **talk sense**, and quite a lot of them **talk nonsense**.

I'**ve got no time for** politicians, and I'm amazed that they imagine we'**re taken in** by some of the things they say.

When they're **in opposition**, they often have good ideas, but when they're **in power** they just seem to **resort to** the same policies that failed last time.

Well, I think, with politicians, **we get what we deserve ▼.**

for my money INF in my opinion.

get a bad/good press receive criticism or praise in newspapers, on TV, etc.

do your best try as hard as you can. SYN try your utmost.

talk down to sb talk to sb as if you think they are not as clever or important as you are.

get on sb's nerves INF make sb angry.

toe the (party) line say or do what sb in authority tells you to say or do, even if you do not agree with it.

believe in sth think that sth is good or right.

talk sense/nonsense/rubbish, etc. INF used to say that you think sb is saying sth that is sensible/stupid, etc.

have (got) no time for sb/sth dislike sb or sth.

take sb in OFTEN PASSIVE trick sb and make them believe sth that is not true.

in opposition a political party that is in opposition is not part of the government of a country. OPP in power.

resort to sth do sth you may not want to do because it is the only course of action that is possible.

WORD FOCUS

In this context, the statement **we get what we deserve** means that we get politicians who are as good or as bad as the people they represent.

Passing laws

In Britain, for a government bill (a proposed new law) to become law, there is first a **long drawn-out** process involving both the House of Commons and House of Lords.

Most bills start in the House of Commons. The first reading **takes place** there, but it is just a formality to tell Members of Parliament (MPs) that a bill is **on its way**. At the second reading, MPs are usually given a day (**as a rule** about six hours) to debate the bill. It then passes to the committee stage. Here, a committee **made up of** 18 to 25 MPs **go through** ▼ the bill, line by line, **in the light of** the debate at the second reading. They may **call in** experts to give evidence, and **put forward** their own amendments. They then **report back to** the Commons.

Further changes can be made at this 'report' stage, and there may be a rebellion by those not **in favour of** the bill. If it **gets through** this stage (it usually does), it has a third reading before being passed to the House of Lords, who then **go through** ▼ a similar process. There may be further amendments, and a bill can go **back and forth** between the two houses for some time before they agree on a final version, and the bill can **go through** ▼.

long drawn-out continuing for a long time, often too long. draw sth out v.
take place happen.
on its/the way happening or arriving soon.
as a rule used to say what usually happens or what is usually true.
make sth up form sth. (Also PASSIVE be made up of sth. SYN consist of sth.)
in the light of sth after considering sth; because of a particular fact.
call sb in ask a person or organization to come and help you.
put sth forward offer an idea, opinion, reason, etc., especially so that people can discuss it and make a decision.
report back (to sb) give sb information about sth that they have asked you to find out about.
in favour (of sth) if you are in favour of sth, you support and agree with it.
get through (sth) be officially accepted or approved.
back and forth from one place to another and back again repeatedly.

WORD FOCUS

There are three different meanings of **go through sth** or **go through** in the text.
1 study and examine something carefully.
2 perform a series of steps or actions.
3 if a bill **goes through**, it becomes law.

19.1 CONCEPTS

Criticism

HANNA I love Leon, but he's always **putting** me **down** in front of everyone. It's almost as if he gets pleasure from **finding fault with** everything I do. I try to **shrug** it **off,** but sometimes it just **gets** me **down**.

SOFIA Yes, I've noticed that. You know, in some ways I think he lacks self-confidence – maybe that's why he **takes it out on** you.

HANNA Hm. I guess I've been quite successful, and I think he **holds** that **against** me.

SOFIA Well, either you've got to **have it out with** him, or just learn to **live with** it.

AXEL You look fed up. Has Otto been **giving you a hard time** again?

SVEN Yes, he **jumped down my throat** this morning when I suggested that we should consider spending less on marketing.

AXEL Well, don't **take** it **personally**. You know what he's like; he's never been good at constructive criticism. He just **lashes out at** people when he's in a bad mood.

SVEN Yeah, I mean, I know he's clever, but he needs to **step back** and **take a long, hard look at** himself. You can't lead a department like that.

put sb down criticize sb, especially in front of other people.

find fault with sb criticize sb, often after trying to find mistakes they have made.

shrug sth off treat sth as if it were unimportant and not worry about it.

get sb down INF make sb feel irritated or depressed.

take sth out on sb make sb suffer because you are angry, upset or tired, even when it is not their fault.

hold sth against sb feel angry with sb because of sth that they have done in the past.

have it out (with sb) talk to sb honestly about a disagreement between you, or sth they have done that is making you angry.

live with sth accept sth unpleasant that you cannot change.

give sb a hard time INF criticize sb a lot or be unpleasant to them.

jump down sb's throat suddenly criticize sb or speak to them very angrily. SYN lash out at sb.

take sth personally get upset because sb is being critical, and you think they are criticizing you in particular.

step back (from sth) think about a situation calmly, as if you are not involved in it.

take a long, hard look at sth/sb think about a problem or issue very carefully in order to find a better way to deal with it.

19.2 CONCEPTS

Dishonesty

When was the last time you told a lie?

JAZEK Mum asked me to take her shopping at the weekend. I **made up** an excuse about work, but she **saw** right **through** it.

HENRIQUE Last night my girlfriend asked me why I was half an hour late. In fact, I'd been buying her birthday present and was trying to **keep** it **from** her, but I had a parcel which kind of **gave the game away**.

RONNIE When I was six, I stole some sweets from a shop. Dad asked me where I'd got them. At first I lied, but eventually I had to **own up**. I should have known I wouldn't **get away with it** – but when you're six, you know nothing!

JO I knew that my brother had broken Mum's favourite vase, but when she asked me who had done it, I didn't **let on**.

When was the last time you were lied to?

ALIONA My brother lied **to my face** about how he got the money. He just thinks he can **pull the wool over** my **eyes**, but I'm not stupid.

OLIVIA Recently a colleague tried to **cover up** a big mistake he'd made with a business deal. I couldn't just **look the other way** – it was serious. Eventually I sat down with him and he **came clean**, but by then it was too late. Stupid, though; he must have known he'd **get found out** ▼.

make sth up invent an explanation for sth, especially to avoid the truth.
see through sth/sb realize that sb is trying to make you believe sth that is not true.
keep sth from sb avoid telling sb sth.
give the game away let people know a secret or surprise which you did not want them to know.
own up (to sth/to doing sth) admit that you are responsible for sth bad or wrong.
get away with sth do sth wrong and not be punished for it.
let on (to sb) INF tell sb sth, especially sth that you have been keeping secret.
to sb's face if you say sth to sb's face, you say it to them directly.
pull the wool over sb's eyes INF trick or deceive sb by not telling them the truth.
cover sth up DISAPPROVING try to stop people from knowing the truth about a mistake, a crime, etc. cover-up N.
look the other way pretend not to see or notice sth bad that is happening. SYN turn a blind eye to sth.
come clean tell the truth about sth bad that you have kept secret.

WORD FOCUS

If you **get** or **are found out**, someone has discovered that you have done something wrong or dishonest. If you **get** or **are caught out**, someone has discovered, often by asking you questions, that you have done something wrong or are lying.

Time

Is time elastic? It must be. My wife **takes forever to** get ready to go out, while I sit there, waiting. The minutes **tick away** … she comes into the living room and appears to be **in no hurry** at all, even though we have to be at our friends' house for 8.00. This all **drags on** for so long that I start to worry that we will never get there **on time** ▼. Somehow, we do.

But apart from moments like that, it seems to me that as I get older, **time flies** – everything is so pressurized. What I would really like to do is to sit down at the weekends, **look back on** what has happened during the week and **take my time to** think things out and **catch up**. But instead, I **rush into** decisions to do with my home life and do everything **at the last minute**.

At work, it's even worse. My boss is terrible with time, so our meetings constantly **run over**, which means I'm **under pressure** the whole time. As a result, I **dash off** my work assignments in a very unsatisfactory way. **One of these days**, I'm going to shout, 'Stop the world! I want to get off!'

take forever (to do sth) take much more time than you would like.

tick away if time ticks away, it passes, especially when you are waiting for sth.

in no hurry (to do sth) not rushed; having plenty of time to do sth.

drag on continue for too long.

time flies used to say that time seems to pass very quickly.

look back on sth think about a time or an event in the past. SYN reflect on sth.

take your time (to do sth) use as much time as you need without hurrying.

catch up spend extra time doing sth because you have not done it earlier.

rush into (doing) sth do sth without thinking about it carefully.

at the last minute at the latest possible time before sth has to happen.

run over (of a meeting, lesson, etc.) continue for longer than planned.

under pressure feeling anxious about sth you have to do, especially when you have too much to do in the time available.

dash sth off write sth very quickly.

one of these days at some time in the near future.

WORD FOCUS

If you are **on time** for something, you arrive at exactly the correct time and are not late. If you are **in time** for something, you arrive before or at the correct time, with time to spare.

Making decisions

Are the statements true for you? ✓ ✗

- ☐ I generally **weigh up** the pros and cons of a situation before making any kind of decision. You'll only **arrive at** the right decision if you **figure** things **out** properly.
- ☐ Once I've **made up my mind** about something, I tend to **stick by** it, **come what may**.
- ☐ I **fell into** my job without **giving it much thought**. I'm very indecisive.
- ☐ I absolutely hate making decisions. My answer is to choose the simplest option and **leave it at that**.
- ☐ I can never **decide on** ▼ what to eat in a restaurant. I keep **changing my mind**, and it drives the waiters mad.
- ☐ When it comes to social activities, I don't have strong feelings. I'm happy to **go along with** what someone else suggests.
- ☐ When I'm choosing a gift for someone, I think it's best to follow my **gut feeling**.
- ☐ I can be impulsive when it comes to buying stuff. If someone offers me something and it's very cheap, I'm likely to **snap** it **up**, **regardless of** whether it's really what I need.

weigh sth up think about the good and bad aspects of sth in order to reach a decision.

arrive at sth make a decision or find a solution, after a lot of effort.

figure sth out think about a problem or situation until you find the answer or understand what has happened.

make up your mind decide sth.

stick by sth do what you decided, promised or planned to do.

come what may despite any problems or difficulties you may have.

fall into sth start doing sth, especially a job, by chance, without having planned it.

give sth some thought think carefully about sth.

leave it at that not do any more about sth.

change your mind change a decision you have made or an opinion you have had.

go along with sth/sb agree with sth/sb.

gut feeling/instinct/reaction INF a feeling or reaction that you are sure is right, although you cannot give a reason for it.

snap sth up INF buy sth very quickly, especially because it is very cheap.

regardless of sth without considering sth.

WORD FOCUS

If you **decide on sth**, you choose it from a number of possible choices. If you **decide against sth**, you decide not to choose it: *I decided against the treatment.*

Success

Do you want to **get ahead** in life? According to successful author and entrepreneur Matthew Toren, you need seven key personality traits for success.

1. Be optimistic: always **look on the bright side**, and just as importantly, don't **dwell on** past failures.
2. Be passionate: find things that will **spur you on** in all aspects of your life.
3. Be persistent: don't **give in**. Everyone **slips up sometime or other**, so just deal with challenges and then **move on**.
4. Be flexible: when the unexpected **crops up**, successful people adapt to change and are prepared to **move with the times**.
5. Educate yourself: even without formal education, people who are prepared to **improve themselves** throughout their lives tend to be more successful.
6. Be focused: everyone wants to **make it** in life, but it's essential to concentrate on the long term. Don't be distracted by the temptation to **make a fast buck**.
7. Be altruistic: really successful people are concerned with others and contributing to the greater good. Helping people and **giving** money **away** ▼ is rewarding.

get ahead be more successful or progress more quickly than other people.

look on the bright side be cheerful or positive about a bad situation.

dwell on sth think or talk a lot about sth, especially sth it would be better to forget.

spur sb on (to sth) encourage sb, or make them want to do sth.

give in stop trying to achieve or win sth.

slip up INF make a careless mistake.

sometime or other at a time in the past or future, but you do not know exactly when.

move on start doing or discussing sth new.

crop up appear or happen, especially when it is not expected.

move with the times change your ideas or behaviour as the world around changes.

improve yourself make yourself a better person, e.g. by learning new skills.

make it be successful in a particular activity, especially your career.

make a fast/quick buck INF, DISAPPROVING earn money quickly and easily.

WORD FOCUS

Give sth away has several meanings:
1 give something to someone, either as a gift or because you no longer need it (see text).
2 tell someone information that you should keep secret: *He gave away military secrets.*
3 in sport, let an opponent win because of your own mistake: *He gave away a goal.*

Making arrangements

From:	Branka Novak
To:	Eleni Andreou
Date:	10 October 2012 12.9.49 GMT+1:00
Subject:	Re: college party

Hi Eleni
I'm trying to **firm up** the arrangements for the college party. Could you **ask around** and see if you can find a band to play that night? **All the best** ▼, Branka

Hi Branka
No problem. It's December 16th, isn't it? If not, **let** me **know** immediately.
Cheers ▼, Eleni

No! I'd hoped to book the hall for the 16th, but that **fell through** so we've **brought** it **forward** to the 5th. B

Sorry to take so long to **get back to** you. I **called in on** Donny last night who would be happy to do it, but we'd have to **fix** it **up with** him soon; he's pretty busy. E

Really sorry, Eleni, but I don't want to use Donny's band. They **got** the dates **mixed up** last year which was a nightmare. I nearly had to **call off** the whole thing. I really don't want to **take** that **risk** again! B firm sth up if you firm up your plans, you make them more final and definite.

ask around speak to different people in order to try and get some information.

no problem INF used to say that you are happy to do sth.

let sb know (sth) tell sb sth.

fall through if a plan, deal or arrangement falls through, it doesn't happen.

bring sth forward move sth to an earlier date or time. OPP put sth back.

get back to sb speak or write to sb again later, especially to give a reply.

call in on sb visit sb, usually for a short time.

fix sth up (with sb) arrange an event, a meeting, etc. with sb.

mix sth up if you mix up the dates of sth, you make a mistake with them. (Also get sth mixed up.) mix-up N.

call sth off if you call sth off, you decide that it will not happen.

take a risk decide to do sth even though you know it may have bad results.

WORD FOCUS

If you are writing an email or letter to a friend, you can end it with **best wishes**, or any of these informal greetings: **all the best**, **cheers** or **take care**.
To a very close friend or relative, you can write **(lots of) love (from)**. To someone you love, you can write **all my love**.

Likes and dislikes

How compatible are you?

We asked Sam and Lily some questions ...

What do you watch on TV?

SAM: I'**m** really **into** rugby, but Lily **can't stand** it! She'**d sooner** watch a ballet, but that just **leaves** me **cold**.

What kind of films do you like?

LILY: I tend to **go for** comedies. Sam's OK with them, but he prefers action films. I think he **revels in** anything violent!

How about music?

LILY: I love The Killers; their last album **blew** me **away**. Sam didn't like it to start with, but it's **growing on** ▼ him.

Do you like the same kind of food?

SAM: Lily'**s mad keen on** Mexican food, but I **can take it or leave it.** And we've both **gone off** ▼ curry; just had too many **takeaways**, I guess!

Do you like each other's friends?

LILY: Sam **took against** my best friend Carly as soon as he met her – which is odd, because she and I **hit it off** straightway. But he's **warming to** ▼ her ... I think!

be into sth INF be interested in an activity or subject and enjoy it.

can't stand sth/sb if you can't stand sth/sb, you dislike it/them very much. SYN can't bear sth/sb.

would sooner do sth = would prefer to do sth. SYN would rather do sth.

leave sb cold if sth leaves sb cold, it does not attract or interest them.

go for sth/sb INF like a particular type of thing or person.

revel in sth enjoy sth very much.

blow sb away INF if sth blows you away, you find it very impressive.

be mad keen on sth/sb INF like sth/sb very much; be very interested in sth/sb.

can take it or leave it INF not care whether you have, see or do sth.

takeaway a meal which you buy in a restaurant and eat at home. take sth away V.

take against sb start not liking sb for no clear reason.

hit it off INF if two people hit it off, they like each other as soon as they meet.

WORD FOCUS

Likes and dislikes can change.
If **sth/sb grows on you**, you start to like it/them more and more.
If you **go off sth/sb** INF, you stop liking it/them.
If you **warm to sb**, you begin to like somebody that you have recently met.

Wants and needs

Complete the questionnaire.

- ☐ **Were** you ever **deprived of** anything when you were a child?
- ☐ Have you ever **had your heart set on** getting something, and then not got it?
- ☐ Do you ever **feel like** giving up what you're doing so that you can travel around the world?
- ☐ Does anyone **depend on** you for help and support?
- ☐ Could you **do without** a car?
- ☐ Have you ever had to **make do with** very little food for a long period of time?
- ☐ Could you live in a tent **if need be**?
- ☐ Is your home **crying out for** ▼ something new or different?
- ☐ Do you ever think you **could do with** a new hairstyle?
- ☐ Do you ever feel **in need of** help with your English?
- ☐ Do you ever think, '**there's no need for** me **to** work as much as I do'?
- ☐ **Have** you **got your eye on** anything you'd like to buy at the moment?
- ☐ Do you ever think, 'I'm **dying for** ▼ a piece of chocolate?'

deprive sb of sth stop sb from having sth, especially sth important.

have your heart set on (doing) sth decide that you want sth very much, especially sth big, important, expensive, etc.

feel like (doing) sth want to have or do sth.

depend on sb/sth need sb/sth in order to be successful or survive.

do without (sth) succeed in living or working without sth.

make do (with sth) manage with the things that you have, even when they are not really enough.

if need be if necessary.

could do with sth INF used to say that you need or would like to have sth.

in need of sth needing sth.

there's no need (for sb) to do sth used to say that sth does not have to be done or should not be done.

have (got) your eye on sth be thinking about sth that you want to have or buy.

WORD FOCUS

A few verbs are usually used in the continuous form.
be crying out for sth INF = need something urgently or very much.
be dying for sth/to do sth INF = want something or want to do something very much.
be starving INF = be feeling very hungry.
be coming up = be about to happen soon: *I've got an exam coming up this week.*

Excuses, excuses

Are you good at **making up** excuses for being late or **taking a day off?** People **phone in** with the most amazing excuses!

The electricity in my flat **went off** for five hours, so the lift was **out of action**. And I live on the 23rd floor.

My five-year old son was **messing around with** my alarm clock, and it didn't **go off**, so I overslept.

Someone in our street **blocked** me **in**, so I couldn't get my car out.

I **got all the way** ▼ to the office then realized I'd **left** my notes **behind**.

I got as far as the entrance and then **walked into** the glass door. My nose hurts.

I put the rubbish out this morning before leaving for work, but I **locked myself out**. Unfortunately I was still in my pyjamas.

My goldfish has died, and I'm not **dealing with** it very well …

Something's **cropped up** at home. It's a bit personal, so I'd rather not **go into** it.

Sorry, but I won't **make it** in today. I **ran out of** petrol on my way to work, and while I was pushing the car to the side of the road, I **did** my back **in**, so I'm at the hospital right now.

make sth up invent sth.
take (time) off have a particular amount of time away from work.
phone in telephone the place where you work to speak to sb or leave a message.
go off **1** (of electricity, lights, etc.) stop working. **2** (of an alarm) ring.
out of action not working or able to be used because of damage or injury.
mess around with sth touch or use sth in a careless way.
block sb in prevent sb from driving away by parking too close to them.
leave sth behind forget to take sth with you.
walk into sth accidentally hit a part of your body against sth when you are walking.
lock yourself out close your front door without having your key with you, so that you are not able to get in again.
deal with sth manage to control your feelings about an emotional problem.
crop up happen unexpectedly.
go into sth talk about sth in detail.
make it be able to be present at a place.
run out of sth use all of sth and not have anything left.
do sth in INF injure a part of your body.

WORD FOCUS

If you say you **went all the way** or **got all the way** to a place, you are emphasizing that you made the journey and it was a waste of time (see text), or that you did it despite a difficulty.

Invitations and offers

A Hi, Jo – listen, do you fancy **coming over** this evening? Sam and I decided we'd **eat in** tonight, and then watch TV **and stuff.**

B I'd love to, but I'**ve got something on** tonight. How about tomorrow?

A What a pity. I've got a council meeting in the evening, and I can't **get out of** it. Look, we'll **invite** you **round** one day next week if that's OK?

C It was really nice **dropping in on** Ali last week – we must **invite** her **back**.

D Yes, either that, or we could **take** her **out** for a meal. She'll insist on **going halves**, but I'd rather we paid.

E I don't feel that Sarah wants to **join in** when we're doing things.

F Well, she'**s** a bit **tied up** at the moment – she's got a lot **on her mind** at work.

G You seem exhausted, Tessa. Can I **help out with** the kids?

H Thanks, but I don't want to **put** you **out** – I can manage at the moment. But I might **take** you **up on** your offer another time!

come over visit sb in the place where they are, especially their home.
eat in have a meal at home, not in a restaurant. OPP eat out.
and stuff INF used to say that there are other things similar to the subject you are discussing.
have (got) something on have arranged to do sth.
get out of sth avoid doing sth that you have promised to do or are expected to do.
invite sb round/over ask sb to come to your home.
drop in on sb make an informal visit to a person or a place.
invite sb back **1** ask sb to come to your home after you have been to their home (see text). **2** invite sb to your home after you have been somewhere together.
take sb out go to a club, restaurant, etc. with sb that you have invited.
go halves (of two people) share the cost of sth equally. SYN go fifty-fifty.
join in do an activity with people who are already doing it.
be tied up be busy.
on your mind if sth is on your mind, you are thinking about it a lot.
help (sb) out (with sth) help sb, especially by doing a particular job or giving sb money.
put sb out cause problems or work for sb.
take sb up on sth accept an offer from sb.

Asking for information

Many people use Google to **find out** what they need to know these days – either for their personal lives, or to **check out** general knowledge facts for quizzes or homework. These are typical questions.

What does DNA **stand for**?

Who was America **named after**?

How can you **tell** crocodiles and alligators **apart**?

How do you **fight off** a shark?

Are humans really **descended from** apes?

How can you tell when fish has **gone off**?

How long can you **go without** water?

How many moons **revolve around** the planet Jupiter?

How much rubbish does the average family **throw away** each year?

How can the government **bring down** the level of unemployment?

How long does it take for a general anaesthetic to **wear off**?

How do you **wire up** a phone socket?

How do I **go about** getting a visa for China?

How can I **opt out of** junk mail?

What qualifications do I need to **go into** advertising as a career?

find sth out get information about sth by asking sb, reading sth, etc.
check sth out examine sth in order to discover whether it is correct.
stand for sth be an abbreviation or symbol of sth.
name sth/sb after sb/sth give sth/sb the same name as another person or thing.
tell sth/sb apart recognize the difference between two people or things that are very similar.
fight sth/sb off stop sth/sb that is attacking you.
be descended from sb be related to sb who lived a long time ago.
go off if food or drink goes off, it becomes bad and should not be eaten or drunk.
go without sth manage without sth that you usually have or need.
revolve around sth move in a circle around sth.
throw sth away get rid of sth that you do not want or need.
bring sth down reduce sth to a lower level.
wear off gradually weaken or stop.
wire sth up connect the wires in a piece of equipment.
go about (doing) sth start dealing with a problem, situation, etc. in a particular way.
opt out (of sth) choose not to take part in sth.
go into sth join an organization or area of activity, especially to start a career in it.

Ways of talking

START TALKING	*She **struck up a conversation with** the passenger opposite.*	strike up a conversation (with sb) start a conversation with sb in an informal way. SYN engage sb in conversation FML.
	*He **chatted** her **up** on the bus!*	chat sb up talk in a friendly way to sb you are romantically attracted to.
SAY STH NEW	*Who **broke the news** about the crash?*	break the news be the first to tell sb some important news.
	*I managed to **slip in** a comment about the no-smoking rule.*	slip sth in say sth without attracting too much attention.
	*He **comes out with** strange things!*	come out with sth say sth unusual or unexpected.
	*Who **brought up** the subject of money – you or your boss?*	bring sth up mention a new subject and start to talk about it.

BAD HABITS	*I hate the way he **talks at** me, rather than talking to me.*	talk at sb talk to sb without letting them say anything.
	*I wish he wouldn't **butt in**; it annoys me.*	butt in rudely interrupt when sb is talking.
	*His voice **trails off** at the end of sentences – I just can't **make out** what he's saying.*	trail off become quieter and stop.
		make sth out OFTEN NEGATIVE hear or understand what sb is saying.
TELLING SECRETS	*I wish I had someone to **confide in** about my problems.*	confide in sb tell sb that you trust about a personal thing, a secret, etc.
	*It was a secret, but he **blurted** it **out**.*	blurt sth out say sth suddenly without thinking.
	*I told her my secret but said, '**Don't breathe a word** about it!'*	not breathe a word keep sth secret. SYN keep quiet about sth, keep sth to yourself.

Conversation rules

Want to be effective in conversation?

Here's how!

- **Oddly enough** ▼, if you want to communicate effectively, you first have to be a good listener. It's essential to **pay attention** when someone else is talking so that you can respond to the other person and keep the conversation going.
- If you're **making** polite **conversation** with someone you don't know well, try to **draw** them **out** by asking about their interests.
- Don't just **take over** the conversation, or you'll **come across as** a dominant bore.
- If you ask someone a question, don't **jump in** with another question before you've heard the answer to the first one.
- Don't **cut** someone **off** in the middle of what they're saying – even if it is boring!
- When it's your turn to speak, provide enough information to **get** your point **across**, but don't **ramble on**.
- If you want to **get through to** people, don't use words they won't know, or long, **drawn-out** sentences. It's far better to **keep it simple**.
- **There's nothing worse than talking over** people: it's very irritating, and no one likes it.

pay attention listen carefully.
make conversation talk to sb that you do not know well, often to be polite.
draw sb out encourage sb to talk and express their feelings.
take sth over if you take over a conversation, you control it by talking and not letting the other person talk.
come across as sth if sb comes across as sth, they create a particular impression, e.g. they seem friendly, boring, cold, etc.
jump in interrupt sb while they are talking.
cut sb off stop sb from continuing what they are saying.
get sth across make sb understand sth.
ramble on talk or write about sth for a long time in a way that is boring or annoying.
get through to sb make sb understand or accept what you say.
drawn-out ADJ lasting longer than is necessary. draw sth out V.
keep it simple avoid making sth difficult or complicated.
there's nothing worse than (doing) sth used to emphasize that sth is unpleasant or not wanted.
talk over sb talk at the same time as another person with the aim of controlling the conversation.

WORD FOCUS

Oddly enough is used to say that something is surprising. You can also say **funnily/strangely/curiously enough**.

Exclamations

Hurry up! We're waiting!
~ **Hang on!** ▼ I'll be there in a minute.

I can't afford to get them a present.
~ **Come off it!** You've got loads of money.

This is too difficult for me.
~ **Come on!** You can do it!

Everything's going wrong at the moment.
~ **Cheer up!** It can't be that bad.

Are you feeling better?
~No, **go away** and **leave me alone!**

I've bought some James Bond cufflinks.
~ Oh, **grow up!**

There's a lorry coming! **Watch out!**

Shut up! I'm trying to work.

Get on with it! We haven't got all day.

What are you doing here? **Push off!**

Take your hands off me!

hurry up! used to tell sb to be quick because there is not much time. SYN get a move on! INF.

come off it! INF used to disagree with sb rudely. SYN don't give me that! INF.

come on! INF used to encourage sb to try harder (see text). It is also used to tell sb that you do not believe what they are saying: *Oh come on! That's not true.*

cheer up! INF used to tell sb to try to be happier.

go away! used to tell sb to leave you.

leave me alone used to tell sb to stop annoying you.

grow up! used to tell sb not to behave in such a silly or childish way.

watch out! INF used to warn sb about sth dangerous. SYNS look out! mind out!

shut up! INF used to tell sb rudely to stop talking.

get on with it! INF used to tell sb in an impatient way to hurry with what they are doing.

push off! INF used to tell sb to go away. SYN clear off! (Both of these phrases are not polite.)

take your hands off me! used to tell sb to stop touching you. SYN get off (me)!

WORD FOCUS

Hang on! INF means 'wait'. SYN **hold on!** It is also used to say that you have just realized something: *Hang on a minute – you didn't give me that money, Dad did!*

Discussion groups

I'm a member of a book group. We **meet up** once a month to discuss a novel we've all agreed to read, but everyone has a different way of **going about** a discussion!

Angela's our leader, and she **draws up** a list of topics for discussion. Often other topics **come up** while we're talking, which is usually OK. She's very good at **drawing out** the quieter people, or those who just **sit back** and do nothing. She **wraps up** the meeting at the end very efficiently.

Pete's quite a difficult member; he **takes issue with** everything, and often **plays devil's advocate**, which I find irritating. He loves to **have the last word**.

Wanda's a bit slow; she often **misses the point** ▼, and I sometimes find that we're talking **at cross purposes**.

Maurice is lovely, but when he's talking, he'll **touch upon** a range of interesting issues but never **get to the point** ▼.

Joanna's clever and often **points out** things that we've missed. She can be very forceful, but she does **talk** a lot of **sense**.

meet up INF (of two or more people) meet each other by arrangement.
go about sth deal with a situation in a particular way.
draw sth up prepare a plan, schedule, etc.
come up be mentioned or discussed.
draw sb out encourage sb to talk or express their feelings.
sit back relax, especially by not doing anything or not getting involved.
wrap sth up INF bring a meeting, lecture, etc. to an end.
take issue with sth/sb start disagreeing with sth or arguing with sb.
play devil's advocate pretend to disagree with sb in order to have an argument or a good discussion with them.
have the last word win an argument by making the last statement on sth.
at cross purposes if two people are at cross purposes, they think they are talking about the same thing, but they are not.
touch on/upon sth mention or talk about a subject without going into detail.
point sth out tell sb sth that they did not already know or had not thought about.
talk sense INF say sth that is sensible.

WORD FOCUS

If you **miss the point**, you don't understand the main thing that somebody is trying to say. If you ask somebody to **get to the point**, you want them to stop talking about details and say what is most important.

Speeches

I would like to thank my parents for **standing by** me during the bad times, and being **a shoulder to cry on**. Making this film has been a difficult task, but we've finally **pulled** it **off**, and we hope it **lives up to** everyone's expectations …

… and now we're married, Ellen and I will **pull together** and deal with any problems that **come our way**. In every decision I make, Ellen always **comes first**; we **rely on** each other totally and know how to …

Of course, I'm sad to be **standing down** after so many years – but it's time for me to **step aside** and **make way for** a younger member of staff. And although I'm **moving on**, I'm happy that …

… so **on behalf of** ▼ the whole staff, we welcome you, Jack, as sales manager, and we **look forward to** working with you in the coming years. We know that you will help us **go from strength to strength** …

stand by sb give sb your help and support when they are in a difficult situation.

a shoulder to cry on sb who listens to your problems and gives you sympathy.

pull sth off INF succeed in doing sth difficult. SYN bring sth off.

live up to sth be as good as what was expected or promised: *live up to expectations.*

pull together act together in an organized way to achieve sth.

come your way if sth comes your way, it happens to you.

come first be the most important person or thing to sb.

rely on sb need or depend on sb.

stand down leave a job or position, especially an important one.

step aside/down leave a job or position, especially so that another person can take your place.

make way for sb let sb take your place.

move on start a new period in your life.

look forward to (doing) sth feel happy and excited about sth that is going to happen.

go from strength to strength become more and more successful.

WORD FOCUS

If you speak **on behalf of** other people, you say for them what they would like to say (see text). If you do something **on behalf of** other people, you help them: *He collected money on behalf of the poor.*

Say it another way 1

The phrasal verbs on the left are more common in spoken English.

PHRASAL VERB	MORE FORMAL EQUIVALENT
If you ***put up with*** *someone's habits,*	you tolerate them. = accept sth unpleasant about them.
If something ***gets*** *you* ***down***, INF	it depresses you. = makes you feel sad or lose hope.
If a bomb ***goes off***,	it explodes. = bursts into pieces with a loud noise.
If you ***turn down*** *an offer,*	you reject it. = refuse to accept it.
If you ***get over*** *a problem,*	you overcome it. = find a way to solve it.
If you ***talk*** *someone* ***into*** *doing something,*	you persuade them to do it. = make them agree to do it by giving them good reasons.
If you ***drop off*** *a parcel at someone's house,*	you deliver it. = take it somewhere and leave it there, then continue your journey.

*If a train **speeds up,***	it accelerates. = moves faster.
*If you **put** someone **down** in front of other people,*	you are disparaging towards them. = make them seem stupid or say that they are wrong.
*If you **take** someone **off,***	you impersonate them. = copy in an amusing way how they speak or behave.
*If you **look up to** someone,*	you respect them. = have a high opinion of them.
*If you **think up** a new system,* INF	you devise or invent it. = create it in your mind.
*If you **put forward** a plan,*	you propose it. = suggest it for discussion.
*If someone attacks you and you **hit back at** them,*	you retaliate. = do sth harmful to them because they have harmed you first.
*If a book **comes out**,*	it is published. = is produced and sold.
*If you **relate to** someone,*	you empathize with them. = are able to understand their situation or how they feel.

Say it another way 2

A Did the boys **confess to** taking the bike?
B Yes, they **owned up** straightaway.
A And were they **expelled**?
B I thought they'd **be kicked out**, but they weren't, luckily for them.

C The cinema's **been demolished**, I hear.
D Yes, it **was pulled down** last week.
C Why didn't they just **renovate** it?
D There was no money to **do** it **up**.

E Robbie's debts are **accumulating**.
F Yes, they've been **mounting up** for years.
E And now the tax office is **investigating**, and they're going to **look into** his affairs.

G The phone company **deceived** us.
H Lots of people **were taken in** by the deal.
G Still, the contract **expires** soon. I think it **runs out** ▼ on the 30th.

I Has the chairman **resigned**?
J They say he's **stood down**, yes.
I So who's going to **deputize for** him?
J I'll be **standing in for** him this month.

K The government is **considering abolishing** cheques.
L They're **thinking of doing away with** cheques? Why on earth would they do that?

own up (to sth/to doing sth) admit that you are responsible for doing sth bad or wrong. SYN confess (to sth/to doing sth).

kick sb out INF make sb leave a school, usually because they have done sth wrong. SYN expel sb.

pull sth down destroy a building, usually because it is very old or damaged. SYNS demolish sth, tear sth down.

do sth up repair and decorate a building, room, etc. SYN renovate sth.

mount up gradually increase in amount. SYN accumulate.

look into sth try to discover the facts about sth such as a problem or a crime. SYN investigate (sth).

take sb in OFTEN PASSIVE make sb believe sth that is not true. SYN deceive sb.

stand down leave a job or position, especially an important one. SYN resign.

stand in for sb temporarily take sb else's place or do their job. SYN deputize for sb.

think of doing sth consider the possibility of doing sth. SYN consider doing sth.

do away with sth INF stop having or allowing sth; make sth end. SYN abolish sth.

WORD FOCUS

If a contract or licence **runs out**, it stops being legal on a certain date (see text). SYN **expire**. If you **run out of sth**, such as money, or something **runs out**, you have none left.

Synonymous phrasal verbs

Two phrasal verbs may have a very similar meaning. The verbs on the left below are generally less frequent and/or more informal than the synonyms on the right.

*I had to **chuck** those vegetables **away** – they were going rotten.*	chuck sth away INF get rid of sth you do not want. SYN throw sth away.
*The wall **is** only **propped up** by a few metal poles.*	prop sth up prevent sth from falling by putting sth under it or against it for support. SYN hold sth up.
*I think Alex wants to **mull** it **over** before he makes a decision.*	mull sth over think carefully about sth over a period of time. SYN think sth over.
*Two of the boys **got ticked off** for missing one of their lessons.*	tick sb off INF speak angrily to sb, especially a child, for doing sth wrong. SYN tell sb off.
*Something **cropped up**, so I'm afraid I couldn't go to the party last night.*	crop up happen or appear, especially unexpectedly. SYN come up.

*My debts have been **mounting up** all year.*	mount up increase gradually in size or quantity. SYN build up.
*The final decision will probably **boil down to** money.*	boil down to sth be the main reason for sth or the most basic part of sth. SYN come down to sth.
*Two of the boys were causing trouble and they **got kicked out**.*	kick sb out (of sth) INF force sb to leave a place or a job. SYN throw sb out (of sth).
*We're almost there with the contract – just one or two things to **iron out**.*	iron sth out deal successfully with a problem, especially as the last part of a process. SYN sort sth out.
*I completely **mucked up** my driving test last week.*	muck sth up INF spoil sth by making a mistake or doing it badly. SYN mess sth up.
*The kids were making a lot of noise. Dan had to tell them to **pipe down**.*	pipe down INF used, especially in orders, to tell sb to stop talking or make less noise. SYN shut up.

Opposites

Someone's planning to **open up** a new bookshop in Compton Street. It's a bit of a risk, really. The last one **closed down** after less than a year.

If I **take out a loan** with this company, I won't have to start **paying** it **back** until next year.

Sian's threatening to **move out** because she's **fallen out with** Jamie again. But she won't do it – they always **make it up** in the end.

I'm always asking Dave to **slow down** when he's driving. I just get so nervous.

I often forget to **log off** when I finish with the computer.

I **took up** judo a while ago, but I had to **give** it **up** after a few months because of a back injury.

The heating **comes on** about six, and **goes off** just after nine.

I thought about **going out** tonight, but it's freezing, so I'm going to **stay in**. Besides, I don't usually **eat out** during the week.

open up/open sth up start (as) a new business. OPP close down/close sth down.

take sth out if you take out a loan, you get official permission to borrow money.

pay sth back return the money that you borrowed.

move out leave your home to live somewhere else. OPP move in.

fall out with sb have an argument with sb so that you are no longer friendly with them. (Also, of two people, fall out.)

make it up (of two people) end a disagreement and become friends again. (Also make up, make (it) up with sb.)

slow down go more slowly. OPP speed up.

log off/out finish using a computer system. OPP log on/in.

take sth up begin doing sth, such as a sport or hobby, regularly.

give sth up stop doing or having sth that you used to do or have regularly.

come on (of electrical appliances) begin to operate. OPP go off.

go out leave your home and go to a cinema, restaurant, etc. for social reasons.

stay in stay at home.

eat out eat in a restaurant. OPP eat in (= eat at home).

WORD FOCUS

If a phrasal verb has another phrasal verb as an opposite or near opposite, it is a good idea to learn the two verbs together, as a pair.

Basic meaning and metaphor

Some phrasal verbs have a basic or literal meaning, but also a more abstract or metaphorical meaning. You can often see a connection between these meanings.

1 I'm afraid I've **broken off** the handle.
2 They've **broken off** their engagement.

1 That old bookcase is **falling apart**.
2 Their marriage is starting to **fall apart.**

1 My feet were **sticking out of** ▼ the bed.
2 This phrase **sticks out** ▼ because it's more informal than the rest of the letter.

1 We can **paper over** this bad bit of wall.
2 If we appoint a new director, we will still be just **papering over the cracks**.

1 The boys were **lined up** against the wall.
2 I have an interview **lined up** for next week.

1 Let's **throw away** these old papers.
2 We **threw away** a two-goal lead.

1 He's too young; he can't **add up** yet.
2 His story just didn't **add up**.

break sth off **1** separate sth using force. **2** end sth such as a relationship.

fall apart **1** be in a very bad condition so that parts break easily. **2** have so many problems that it is no longer possible to exist or function.

paper over sth **1** use wallpaper on a wall to cover and hide sth. **2** if you paper over the cracks, you try to hide a problem or disagreement in a way that is temporary and will probably not be successful.

line sb/sth up **1** arrange people or things in a straight line or row. **2** arrange for an activity or event to happen.

throw sth away **1** get rid of sth you no longer want, for example by putting it in a bin. **2** waste sth such as an opportunity or advantage, for example by doing sth stupid.

add up **1** calculate the total of several numbers or amounts. **2** OFTEN NEGATIVE seem reasonable or true.

WORD FOCUS

1 If something **sticks out (of sth)**, it comes out further than the other parts on a surface: *His ears stick out. She stuck her tongue out.*
2 If something **sticks out,** you notice it because it is unusual, different, or better/worse than other things, etc. SYN **stand out**.
If something **sticks out a mile**, it is very noticeable. If something **sticks in sb's mind**, they remember it well.

Metaphorical meaning

Some phrasal verbs only have a metaphorical meaning. They can be difficult to understand without a clear context.

I was just **drifting off** when the phone rang.

He just **brushed off** the journalist's suggestion that he was lying.

After that mistake, I mustn't **slip up** again.

His mother **passed away** in the night.

I try to forget what happened that day, but the memories keep **flooding back**.

Why are those guys **nosing around** the office at the moment?

Mel keeps **plugging away at** her Spanish, but it's slow progress.

We **stumbled across** an interesting little art gallery while we were there.

I was climbing over a fence and my back just **seized up**.

He **swears by** whisky to cure a cold.

I **scraped through** the exam.

He said he'd marry her, but I think he's just **stringing** her **along** ▼.

drift off start to sleep: *drift off to sleep.*
brush sb/sth off refuse to listen to sb or their ideas, especially in a rude way.
slip up INF make a careless mistake.
pass away die. (This word is used to avoid saying 'die' when you think it might upset someone.)
flood back if memories or feelings flood back, you suddenly remember them very clearly.
nose around/about sth look around a place to try to find sth, especially information.
plug away (at sth) continue doing sth in a determined way, but with difficulty.
stumble across/on sth/sb find sth or meet sb by accident.
seize up stop moving or working correctly.
swear by sth NOT USED IN THE CONTINUOUS FORM say that you are certain that sth is good or effective.
scrape through (sth) succeed in doing sth such as passing an exam, but doing it with difficulty and not doing it well.

WORD FOCUS

If you **string sb along** INF, you make them continue believing something that is not true, especially about your intentions or beliefs (see text).
If you **string along (with sb)** INF, you go somewhere with somebody, especially because you have nothing else to do: *If you're going out, do you mind if I string along?*

Informal phrasal verbs

Blogspot: Get it off your chest!

RIP-OFF

Everything's going badly at the moment. Last weekend I bought a second-hand car – big mistake – it's **packed up** already. I knew the dealer was **ripping** me **off**, but I just went ahead anyway! What's wrong with me???
Angry Dave

LOYAL FRIENDS?

I **ran into** an old friend on holiday in Greece last summer, and I agreed to **look** him **up** when we were back home. We were supposed to **get together** last weekend, but he just kept **mucking** me **about**, changing the time and place several times. He finally **rolled up** two hours late, **stuck around** for half an hour, then he just **took off**. Is that the way to treat old friends? *FedupFred*

BIG BAD BOSS

I have a terrible boss; nobody can stand him. We're all **beavering away** in the office, then suddenly he appears at the door and **pulls** someone **up** for a minor mistake. No one likes **being shown up** in front of their colleagues. I'm starting to hate this job – I'm going to **pack** it **in** if things don't **look up** soon. *Livid Lily* pack up INF (of a machine or piece of equipment) stop working.

rip sb off INF cheat sb by making them pay too much or selling them sth of poor quality. rip-off N, INF.

run into sb INF meet sb by accident. SYN bump into sb INF.

look sb up INF go to see sb you have not met for a long time, usually when you are visiting the place where they live.

get together INF (of two or more people) meet socially.

muck sb about INF treat sb badly, especially by changing your mind a lot.

roll up INF arrive somewhere late.

stick around INF stay in a place for a period of time.

take off INF leave a place suddenly or in a hurry.

beaver away (at sth) INF work very hard, especially at writing or calculating sth.

pull sb up INF criticize sb for sth they have done wrong.

show sb up INF embarrass sb.

pack sth in INF stop doing an activity or a job.

look up INF become better; improve.

WORD FOCUS

The phrasal verbs in this unit are all very informal, and more likely to be used in spoken English and informal written English.

More formal phrasal verbs

There are a small number of more formal phrasal verbs. These are normally used in written English or formal spoken English such as broadcasts, debates, lectures, etc.

As the President **embarks on** his second term in office, he knows he will have to **contend with** a number of extremely difficult issues, not least of which is the fact that he will be **presiding over** a country in the grip of an economic recession.

The opposition are **resigning themselves to** another four years without power, and may soon **engage in** their own internal battle for leadership.

My client will **adhere to** the terms of his probation; I can **vouch for** that.

I have already **alluded to** the fact that we may have to **dispense with** ▼ a number of bus services in rural areas.

The company do not **subscribe to** the view that they are being irresponsible. Nevertheless, they are not keen to **dwell on** the subject of exactly how they **dispose of** the waste.

embark on/upon sth FML start to do sth new or difficult.

contend with sth have to deal with a problem or difficult situation.

preside over sth/sb be in a position of power over a country or group of people, especially while important changes or events are happening.

resign yourself to sth accept sth bad or harmful that cannot be changed or avoided.

engage in sth FML take part or be involved in sth.

adhere to sth FML obey a law, rule, agreement, etc. SYN abide by sth FML.

vouch for sth FML say that you believe sth is true. (Also vouch for sb say that you believe sb will behave well.)

allude to sth FML mention sth indirectly.

subscribe to sth FML agree with or support an opinion, a theory, etc.

dwell on/upon sth talk or think about sth, especially sth that it would be better to forget about.

dispose of sth/sb get rid of sth/sb that you do not want or cannot keep.

WORD FOCUS

If you **dispense with sth**, you stop having it or using it because you no longer need it or cannot afford it (see text).

If you **dispense with sb's services**, you stop employing them or you dismiss them from their job.

Back

When **back** is used in phrasal verbs, it usually has the sense of 'returning' or 'returning something'.

I only borrowed the money. I'll have to ***pay*** *it* ***back*** *by the end of the month.*

The books weren't the ones I ordered, so I ***sent*** *them* ***back****.*

Cathy left a message on my answerphone. I'll ***ring*** *her* ***back*** *later.*

Put *the books* ***back*** *when you've finished.*

I had to pay a deposit, but I should ***get*** *it* ***back*** *when I leave the flat.*

We ought to try and ***get back to*** ▼ *the flat before the others arrive.*

Do you often ***look back on*** *your childhood?*

It was getting dark, so we decided to ***turn back****.*

Other verbs like this are: *come back, go back, take sth back, bring sth back* and *give sth back.*

A few verbs with **back** do not have this sense of returning or returning something.

I've been spending a lot recently. I may have to ***cut back*** *a bit.*

Mark has problems with reading; his teacher thinks it's ***holding*** *him* ***back****.*

That boy always ***answers back****, whatever you say to him.*

pay sth back return money that you borrowed from sb.

send sth back return sth that sb sent you, especially by post, and often because it is not satisfactory.

ring sb back phone sb who phoned you earlier. SYNS call sb back, phone sb back.

put sth back return sth to its usual place, or the place where it was before it was moved.

get sth back have sth returned to you after it has been lost or taken from you.

look back on sth think about a time or an event in your past.

turn back turn round and return the way you came.

cut back reduce the amount of sth that you use or spend.

hold sb back stop sb from being as successful as they should.

answer (sb) back reply rudely to sb who has more authority than you, especially when they are criticizing you or telling you to do sth.

WORD FOCUS

Get back to sth or **sb** has different meanings.

1 return to a place (see text).

2 return to an earlier state or condition: *I woke at five o'clock, and couldn't get back to sleep.*

3 speak or write to somebody later, especially to give a reply: *I don't know if I'm free, but I'll get back to you soon.*

Through

When **through** is used in phrasal verbs, it often gives the sense of doing something from beginning to end.

*I **slept through** the storm without waking.*

*It must've been awful for the people who **lived through** the war.*

*I always **read through** my English essays to check for spelling and grammar mistakes.*

*We'll have to **look through** the files to see what's in there.*

*I **flicked through** the magazine but I couldn't find anything of interest.*

*I hope we can **get through** ▼ the course book by the end of this term.*

*Mr Phillips **took** us **through** the ordering process before we had to do it on our own.*

*We've got some way to go with this project, but it's important to **see** it **through**.*

Occasionally **through** does not have this meaning in a phrasal verb.

*She was trying to arrange a date for me, but I could **see through** her little game.*

*The protesters **broke through** the barrier.*

sleep through sth remain sleeping even though there is a lot of noise around you.

live through sth experience a dangerous or unpleasant situation that lasts for several years.

read through sth read sth from beginning to end to check or correct it.

look through sth examine or read sth quickly, often to look for information.

flick through sth turn the pages of a book, newspaper, etc. very quickly, looking briefly at some of the pages.

take sb through sth show or explain to sb how to do sth from beginning to end.

see sth through continue doing sth until it is finished.

see through sth/sb realize that sb is trying to make you believe sth that is not true: *see through sb's little game.*

break through sth manage to get past or through something that is in your way by using force.

WORD FOCUS

Get through has a number of different meanings.

1 get through sth manage to do or complete something (see text).

2 get through (sth) be successful in an exam: *It was a difficult exam but they all got through.*

3 get through (to sb) make contact with somebody by phone: *I tried to ring you but I couldn't get through.*

Around, about

In phrasal verbs, **around** often expresses the idea of doing something in a relaxed way, or without any particular purpose. You can also use **about** in many of these verbs.

*You often see gangs of boys **hanging around** the city centre at night.*

*If it's hot, we'll probably just **laze around** the pool this afternoon.*

*She should be looking for a job, but she just **lies around** ▼ the house all day.*

*My husband was **messing around** in the garden while I did most of the shopping.*

*The teacher had to tell the two boys three times to stop **messing about** and get on with their work.*

Some phrasal verbs with **around** express the idea of going to different places.

*We decided to **look around** the village before we had something to eat.*

*With the new underground it's easy to **get around** the city.*

*I often **shop around** before buying clothes.*

*I had to **show** some of the new students **around** the school.*

*I used to **go around with** Judy a lot when I was at college.*

*We've been **rushing around** all day, getting things ready for the holiday.*

hang around/about INF spend time in a place, not doing very much.
laze around/about relax and enjoy yourself, doing no work.
mess around/about INF **1** spend time doing sth for pleasure, in a very relaxed way. **2** behave in a stupid way, doing things which are not important.
look around/round walk round a building or place to see what is there.
get around/round/about (sth) move from place to place within an area.
shop around (for sth) go to different shops to compare quality and prices before buying anything.
show sb around/round sth take sb to all the different parts of a place when they visit it for the first time.
go around with sb spend a lot of time with sb, going to different places and doing different things.
rush around/about try to do a lot of things or go to a lot of places in a short time.

WORD FOCUS

Lie around can mean to spend time being lazy when you should be doing something (see text), or it can mean simply relaxing: *We lay around all afternoon in the sun.*
It can also be used when something has been left somewhere in an untidy or careless way, and not put in the correct place: *My teenage son leaves his clothes lying around on the floor.*

On

With a number of phrasal verbs, the particle **on** adds the sense of something continuing.

We heard the alarm about 11 o'clock; it ***went on*** ▼ *for ages.*

I ***keep on*** *getting headaches. I think I may have to go and see the doctor about them.*

Brad was thinking of leaving, but he's decided to ***stay on*** *for another year.*

I'm going to stop for lunch, then I must ***get on with*** *some work.*

I thought it was going to be a short meeting, but it ***dragged on*** *for ages.*

We ***carried on*** *working until it was dark.*

Take one of these ***handouts****, then* ***pass*** *them* ***on****.*

I don't want to stop yet. Let's ***drive on*** *until we get to the next service station.*

There are also many phrasal verbs where **on** does not have this meaning.

My brother is always ***picking on*** *me.*

We plan to ***take on*** *more staff.*

The building work is really ***coming on*** *now; it'll soon be finished.*

keep (on) doing sth continue doing sth or do the same thing many times.
stay on remain at a job, school or place for longer than you planned.
get on with sth continue doing sth after an interruption.
drag on continue for longer than you want or think is necessary.
carry on (doing sth) continue doing sth.
handout a free piece of paper with printed information on it, often given to students in a class or people at a lecture, or used to advertise sth. hand sth out v.
pass sth on (to sb) give sth to someone else, after receiving it or using it yourself.
drive on continue driving.
pick on sb treat sb unfairly, by blaming, criticizing or punishing them.
take sb on employ sb.
come on make progress.

WORD FOCUS

Go on can mean to continue without stopping (see text). It also has other meanings with a sense of something continuing:
1 USUALLY IN THE CONTINUOUS happen: *What's going on in here?*
2 continue speaking, often after a pause: *Please go on with your story.*
3 (of time) pass or continue: *I just got more and more tired as the evening went on.*

Up

In some phrasal verbs, the particle **up** adds emphasis to the base verb, but does not change the meaning.

*What time did you **wake up**?*

***Stand up** and wait over there.*

You can use many of these verbs with or without the particle.

*Please **hurry (up)**.*

*I had to **chop (up)** all the onions.*

*We had to **queue (up)** for tickets.*

*Can you **serve (up)** the food now?*

Some phrasal verbs with **up** add the idea of completing or finishing something.

***Drink up**, then we can go.*

*The kids **finished up** the chicken.*

*We managed to **wind up** the meeting early.*

*Could you **tidy up** your room?*

*Can you help me **load up** the car?*

Some phrasal verbs with **up** describe something increasing or getting larger.

*We'll have to **put up** our prices soon.*

*My debts are **mounting up**.*

*My work has been **piling up** recently.*

*The pressure has been **building up** ▼ for ages; the boss may decide to quit.*

wake up stop sleeping.
stand up rise to your feet from sitting or lying.
hurry up do sth or move somewhere quickly.
chop sth up cut sth, especially food, into smaller pieces.
queue up wait in a line of people to do sth, have sth, or go somewhere.
serve (sth) up put food onto a plate for people to eat.
drink (sth) up drink all of sth.
finish sth up eat, drink or use what remains of sth.
wind sth up bring sth such as a meeting or speech to an end.
tidy sth up make a room, desk, etc. look better by putting everything in order.
load (sth) up put a large quantity of things into sth such as a vehicle, dishwasher, etc.
put sth up increase the price of sth.
mount up increase gradually in size or quantity.
pile up become larger in size or quantity.

WORD FOCUS

If something **builds up**, it increases in size, quantity or strength (see text).
build-up N.
If you **build sth up**, you successfully develop it over time: *She's built up a successful company.*

Off

Off is used in some phrasal verbs to express the idea of somebody or something leaving.

*The plane **takes off** at six o'clock.*

*My parents are going to New York. I'll probably go to the airport to **see** them **off**.*

*We **set off** for the mountains at midday.*

*We were on private land and the owner told us to **clear off**.*

*I can usually **get off** work early on Fridays.*

*The referee **sent** the player **off** for a dangerous tackle.*

*Sarah's **gone off to** have lunch.*

*There's a small road at Porlock that **branches off** to the sea at West Porlock.*

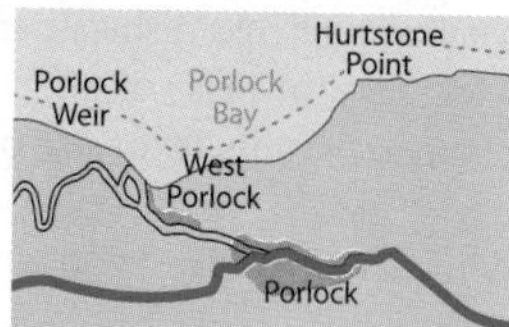

Off can express the idea of removing or separating something.

*We **cut off** a large branch from that tree.*

*Our village **was cut off** during the floods.*

*Why don't you **take** your jacket **off**?*

*The police have **cordoned off** the embassy.*

*I **broke off** ▼ a bit of chocolate and ate it.*

take off (of an aircraft) leave the ground and begin to fly.

see sb off go somewhere such as an airport or station with sb, so that you can say goodbye to them when they leave.

set off leave a place in order to start a journey, especially a long journey.

clear off used to tell sb rudely to go away.

get off sth leave the place where you work at the end of the day: *get off work/duty.*

send sb off (in football or rugby) order sb to leave the pitch because they have broken the rules.

go off (to do sth) leave a place in order to do sth.

branch off if a small road or part of a river branches off, it leaves the main road or main part of the river (see picture).

cut sth off **1** remove sth from sth larger by cutting. **2** OFTEN PASSIVE make a place impossible to leave or enter, or break a means of communication.

take sth off remove sth, especially a piece of clothing.

cordon sth off stop people from getting into an area by surrounding it with police, soldiers, etc.

WORD FOCUS

If you **break sth off**, you separate something using force (see text). We can use the same verb to describe ending a relationship: *They got engaged in the spring, but Claire broke it off.*

Get

Heard around the office

The new boss is **getting along** well.

OK, I know salaries are important, but we can't **get into** that right now.

Robert can't expect to **get on** in life if he doesn't **get in** on time in the morning.

My boss **got** me **through** the first difficult year, and without him I would have left.

I kept meaning to write that report, but I never **got round to** it.

There are a lot of employment regulations, but the company seems to **get round** them.

The news that John had resigned **got around** in no time. I think people will be sorry to see him go.

I've got an interview today. I'll be glad to **get** it **over with.**

Right, it's time we **got onto** the next point on the agenda.

The photocopier's broken again. I'll have to **get onto** technical support.

The documents are in a locked cupboard; I can't **get at** ▼ them.

get along (with sth) make progress in a situation.

get into sth INF become involved in sth, such as a discussion.

get on be successful in your career, etc.: *get on in life.*

get in arrive at a place.

get sb through sth help sb deal with or live through a difficult situation or period.

get round to (doing) sth do sth that you have been intending to do for a long time.

get round sth find ways to avoid doing sth that causes problems for you, or that is difficult.

get around if news or information gets around, a lot of people hear it.

get sth over with INF do or finish sth that is difficult or that you do not want to do.

get onto sth start talking about a new subject after discussing sth else.

get onto sb contact sb in order to ask them to do sth for you.

WORD FOCUS

If you cannot **get at** something, it means you cannot reach it or touch it (see text).
If someone keeps **getting at** you INF, it means they are always criticizing you.
If someone wants to **get at** the truth, they are trying to discover the true facts about something.

Go

A number of phrasal verbs with **go** are connected to different kinds of movement.

I'm planning to ***go down to*** *Brighton tomorrow.*

I'm just ***going round to*** *my sister's.*

There's a rumour ***going around*** *that they're getting married.*

The woman seemed to be on her own, so I ***went over*** *and introduced myself.*

The top two teams in the league ***go up*** *every year.*

You ***go ahead*** *and we'll follow on later.*

There are also phrasal verbs with **go** which are often used with particular nouns to form idiomatic phrases.

Speaking a foreign language gets easier as ***time goes by****.*

The council has given us a summary of the report, but they won't ***go into detail****.*

If my father promised to help you, I'm sure he will. He never ***goes back on his word****.*

We've just been ***going round in circles*** *with this new scheme.*

It was terrifying; the whole building just ***went up in flames****.*

I'm pleased to say that the ceremony ***went off▼ without a hitch****.*

It took ages for the kids to ***go off▼ to sleep****.*

go down (to ...) go from one place to another, especially to somewhere further south. OPP go up (to ...).
go around/round (to ...) visit a person or a place that is near.
go around/round (of a rumour, a story, gossip, etc.) be passed from person to person.
go over (to ...) move from one place to another, especially when it means crossing sth such as a room, a city, etc.
go up if a sports team goes up, it moves from a lower league to a higher league.
go ahead travel in front of other people in your group to arrive before them.
go by if time goes by, it passes.
go into detail explain sth fully.
go back on your word fail to do sth that you promised or agreed to do.
go round in circles work at sth or discuss sth in detail without making any progress.
go up in flames start burning quickly or explode.

WORD FOCUS

If an organized event **goes off without a hitch**, it happens without any problems (see text).
If somebody **goes off to sleep**, they start to sleep (see text).
If a **bomb goes off**, it explodes: *The bomb went off without any warning.*
If a **gun goes off**, it is fired: *The gun just went off while he was cleaning it.*

Take

*If you **take** something **up with** someone,*	you speak or write to them about something that they can help you with or deal with.
*If you **are taken up with** your job or your interests,*	you give all your time or energy to them.
*If someone is explaining something to you, and you can't **take** it **in**,*	you cannot understand and remember it.
*If you **take** your trousers **in**,*	you make them tighter because they are too big. (If you take them up, you make them shorter.)
*If you hear a piece of music and it **takes** you **back** to your childhood,*	the music makes you remember something in the past.
*If you **are taken aback** by something that someone says or does to you,*	you are surprised or shocked by it.

If you ***take*** *a piece of equipment* ***apart****,*	you separate it into different parts.
If you ***take*** *an opposing team* ***apart****,* INF	you defeat them easily in a game.
If your career suddenly ***takes off****,*	you start to become successful.
If you ***take yourself off*** *somewhere,* INF	you leave a place and go somewhere else.
If you suddenly ***take to*** *gett****ing*** *up early in the morning,*	you start getting up early as a habit.
If you ***take to*** *something* ***like a duck to water****,*	you learn to do it very easily, as if you have been doing it for a long time.
If you ***take*** *a fence* ***down****,*	you remove it by separating it into pieces.
If you ***take*** *an address* ***down****,*	you write it down.

Come

*I think her work is **coming along** well.*

*The man **came at** me with a knife; I was terrified.*

*A lot of the fruit we eat **comes from** South Africa.*

*Good jobs are very hard to **come by** at the moment.*

*I don't want my job to **come between** us.*

*I took the job because it sounded exciting – money didn't **come into** ▼ it.*

*A man **came up to** me and asked me if I wanted to dance.*

There are a number of phrasal verbs with **come** that have two particles.

*We **came up against** a lot of opposition from residents when we tried to change the parking regulations.*

*It's a difficult decision, but I think it **comes down to** who wants the job most.*

*I **came away with** the impression that things weren't going well.*

*The government has **come in for** a lot of criticism.*

*Can we **come back to** this topic later?*

*Their little boy **comes out with** some very strange remarks.*

come along USUALLY IN THE CONTINUOUS make progress, or get better in quality, skill or health. SYN come on.

come at sb suddenly move towards sb as if you are going to attack them.

come from sth be made in or obtained from a particular place.

come by sth manage to find or obtain sth.

come between sb and sb damage a relationship between two people.

come up (to sb) move towards sb in order to talk to them.

come up against sth/sb be faced with problems or be opposed by sb.

come down to sth be decided by sth which is the most important aspect of a situation.

come away with sth leave a place with a particular feeling or impression: *come away with the impression that …*

come in for sth receive sth, especially criticism: *come in for criticism.*

come back to sth return to sth that you were discussing or dealing with earlier.

come out with sth say sth, especially sth surprising or unusual.

WORD FOCUS

Come into sth is used in different ways.
1 be important in a particular situation (see text).
2 if you **come into sth**, it becomes yours when someone dies: *Anna came into a fortune when her father died.*

Turn

There are a number of verbs and idioms with **turn** whose meaning involves some kind of change: a change in direction, a change of position, a change from one state to another, etc.

*If you heat ice, it **turns into** water.*	turn (sth) into sth change (or make sth change) into sth different.
***Turn** the picture **around** so that I can see it.*	turn sth around/round move sth so that it faces the other way.
*I'm trying to speak to Elle – could you **turn** the TV **down**?*	turn sth down reduce the sound, heat, etc. of a piece of equipment. OPP turn sth up.
*Can we **turn over** and watch the film now?*	turn over change to another channel when you are watching television.
*Cook the meat on one side, then **turn** it **over** after half an hour.*	turn sth over make sth change position so that the other side is facing towards the outside or the top.

Example	Meaning
*The skirt was too long, so I **turned** it **up**.*	turn sth up change the length of a skirt, trousers, etc. by folding the bottom part up and sewing it. OPP let sth down.
*When he left prison, Steven promised he would **turn over a new leaf**.*	turn over a new leaf change your way of life to become a better, more responsible person.
*The new employment law will **turn the clock back** 100 years.*	turn the clock back cause things to be done the way they were done in the past.
*That illness has **turned** him **into** an old man.*	turn (sb) into sth become (or make sb become) a different kind of person.
*She **turned** the whole family **against** him.*	turn sb against sb make sb stop being friendly towards sb.
*My sister's life has **been turned upside down** by the accident.*	turn sb's life/world upside down change sb's life completely, often in a negative way.

Put

*Could you **put** the kettle **on**?*

*She **puts** her success **down to** hard work.*

*A lift to the station would be great, but I don't want to **put** you **out** ▼.*

*I'm not **putting myself out for** ▼ him again – he never says thank you.*

*Did they manage to **put** the fire **out**?*

*The residents are **putting up** a great fight to prevent the closure of the post office.*

*I've got a meeting in London on Tuesday. Could you **put** me **up** for the night?*

There are also a number of idioms with **put** + noun + preposition + noun.

*The doctors are **putting pressure on** the government over the health reforms.*

*He's disappointed he didn't get a place, but he's trying to **put a brave face on it**.*

*You're **putting words into my mouth**. That's not what I meant at all.*

***Put yourself in my place**; what could I have done?*

*Don't **put all your eggs in one basket** – I would apply for as many jobs as you can.*

*I **put money on** two horses, and they both lost.*

*José told me to speak to Mandy. Apparently, she'll **put** me **in the picture** about the party.*

put sth on switch on a piece of electrical equipment.

put sth down to sth consider sth as the reason for sth else. (In this case, hard work is the reason for her success.)

put sth out stop a fire from burning.

put up sth be involved in a fight or struggle to achieve sth or prevent sth: *put up a fight/resistance.*

put sb up let sb stay in your home, usually for a night or several nights.

put pressure on sb (to do sth) force or try to persuade sb to do sth.

put a brave face on it try to hide the fact that you are feeling upset or disappointed.

put words into sb's mouth claim that sb has said sth, when in fact they did not say it, or they meant sth different.

put yourself in sb's place/position imagine yourself in sb else's situation.

put all your eggs in one basket rely on one course of action for success rather than giving yourself different possibilities.

put money on sth INF gamble money on the result of a game, race, etc.

put sb in the picture INF give sb information that they need to understand sth.

WORD FOCUS

If you **put sb out**, you cause difficulties or problems for them. If you **put yourself out (for sb)** INF, you make a special effort to do something for them.

Keep

I'm a grandmother now, and my daughter Jenny and I sometimes have different ideas about bringing up children. For instance, my grandchildren eat a lot of sweets, but in my day, I **kept** my kids **off** sugary foods. I also tried to **keep** them **busy** with endless outdoor activities; they were running about in the fields all day. But with my grandchildren, it's completely different – it's hard to **keep** them **away from** their computers and mobile phones. I know it **keeps** them **quiet**, but I'd rather they were out playing, not stuck indoors all day!

And that's another problem I didn't have: Jenny really has to **keep an eye on** what they're doing on their computers, because they don't understand the dangers. I can't **keep up with** all this new technology, but if you're a parent these days, you have to.

But I will say this – Jenny's much better at **keeping** her temper **in check** than I was. The kids argue a lot, but she tries to **keep out of** it and lets them sort things out for themselves. Mind you, she can be very strict – on one occasion, she **kept** Jack **in** all weekend because he'd been naughty.

It's hard bringing up kids, but I know she tries to **keep to** ▼ her rules, which is the right thing to do. She's a great mum!

keep (sb) off sth avoid (or make sb avoid) a particular type of food or drink.

keep sb busy give sb a lot of things to do or to think about, often as a way of filling time.

keep sb away (from sth) make sb avoid going somewhere, doing sth, or using sth.

keep sb quiet stop sb from talking, complaining or causing trouble.

keep an eye on sth/sb take care of sth/sb and make sure that they are not harmed, damaged, etc.

keep up with sth continue to read or learn about a particular subject so that you always know the most recent facts, products, etc.

keep/hold sth in check keep sth under control so that it does not get worse or spread.

keep out of sth not become involved in sth.

keep sb in make sb stay indoors or in a particular place.

WORD FOCUS

If you **keep to** a rule or an agreement, you do what you have been instructed, or have promised or agreed, to do (see text).
If you **keep to** a path or road, you stay on it and do not leave it.
If you **keep to the point**, you write or talk only about the particular subject you are supposed to talk or write about.

Irregular verbs

This is a selection of irregular verbs, based on verbs and derivatives in this book.

Base form	Past tense	Past participle
abide	abided	abided
be	was, were	been
bear	bore	borne
beat	beat	beaten
bend	bent	bent
blow	blew	blown
break	broke	broken
bring	brought	brought
build	built	built
burn	burnt, burned	burnt, burned
burst	burst	burst
buy	bought	bought
catch	caught	caught
come	came	come
cut	cut	cut
deal	dealt	dealt
do	did	done
draw	drew	drawn
dream	dreamt, dreamed	dreamt, dreamed
drink	drank	drunk
drive	drove	driven
dwell	dwelled, dwelt	dwelled, dwelt
eat	ate	eaten
fall	fell	fallen
feel	felt	felt
fight	fought	fought

Base form	Past tense	Past participle
find	found	found
fit	fitted, fit	fitted, fit
get	got	got
give	gave	given
go	went	gone
grow	grew	grown
hang	hung	hung
have	had	had
hear	heard	heard
hit	hit	hit
hold	held	held
keep	kept	kept
lay	laid	laid
lead	led	led
leave	left	left
let	let	let
lie	lay	lain (rare)
lose	lost	lost
make	made	made
meet	met	met
pay	paid	paid
put	put	put
read /ri:d/	read /red/	read /red/
ring	rang	rung
run	ran	run
see	saw	seen
sell	sold	sold
send	sent	sent
set	set	set
shake	shook	shaken
show	showed	shown
shut	shut	shut
sing	sang	sung
sink	sank	sunk

Base form	Past tense	Past participle
sit	sat	sat
sleep	slept	slept
speak	spoke	spoken
speed	speeded, sped	speeded, sped
spell	spelt, spelled	spelt, spelled
spill	spilt, spilled	spilt, spilled
split	split	split
spread	spread	spread
stand	stood	stood
stick	stuck	stuck
strike	struck	struck
string	strung	strung
sweep	swept	swept
take	took	taken
tear	tore	torn
tell	told	told
think	thought	thought
throw	threw	thrown
wake	woke	woken
wear	wore	worn
win	won	won
wind	wound	wound
write	wrote	written

Key to symbols

Phonetic symbols (in the wordlist)

iː	tea	ʊ	book	əʊ	so
ɪ	sit	uː	fool	aʊ	now
i	happy	u	actual	ɔɪ	boy
e	ten	ʌ	cup	ɪə	dear
æ	had	ɜː	bird	eə	chair
ɑː	car	ə	away	ʊə	sure
ɒ	dog	eɪ	pay		
ɔː	ball	aɪ	cry		
p	put	f	first	h	house
b	best	v	van	m	must
t	tell	θ	three	n	next
d	day	ð	this	ŋ	song
k	cat	s	sell	l	love
g	good	z	zoo	r	rest
tʃ	cheese	ʃ	ship	j	you
dʒ	just	ʒ	pleasure	w	will

(r) shows a linking r, pronounced before a vowel but (in British English) not before a consonant

ˈ precedes a stressed syllable

Other symbols

The symbol / (forward slash) between two words or phrases means that either is possible.

We also use slashes around phonetic symbols, e.g. *tea* /tiː/.

Brackets ( ) around a word or phrase in an example mean it can be left out.

~ means that there is a change of speaker.

▼ is a reference to the word focus where there is more information.

Abbreviations used in this book

N	noun
V	verb
ADJ	adjective
OPP	opposite
SYN	synonym
INF	informal
FML	formal
PL N	plural noun
PT	past tense
PP	past participle
sth	something
sb	somebody
etc.	You use 'etc.' at the end of a list to show there are other things, but you aren't going to say them all.
i.e.	that is
e.g.	for example

Acknowledgements

The authors and publisher are grateful to those who have given permission to reproduce the following extracts and adaptations of copyright material:

p34 Adapted from 'How to Understand the Mother and Daughter Relationship', *Daily Mail*, 1 June 2006. Copyright Deborah Tannen. Reprinted with permission.
p38 Extract from 'Danger: friends at work' by Helena Jaworski-Lang, *The Independent*, 15 August 1999. Reproduced by permission.
p206 Extract from 'How to be Successful at All You Do - 7 Crucial Personality Traits' by Matthew Toren, Blogtrepeneur.com. Reproduced by permission.

Authors' acknowledgements

We are greatly indebted to Amanda Holmbrook and Julia Elliott for their expert advice and careful editing of the manuscript.

We would like to thank the following for permission to reproduce photographs:

Alamy Images pp12 (Old trainers/Hugh Threlfall), 22 (Nurse with patient/Blend Images), 42 (Couple at home/moodboard), 66 (Farmer/Stockbroker), 70 (Taxi/Alvey & Towers Picture Library), 72 (Angry driver/UK Stock Images Ltd), 114 (Marathon runners/Liz Finlayson), 124 (Sledging/Mark Boulton), 138 (Newlyweds/MARKA), 146 (Flood/Travel and Landscape UK/Mark Sykes), 150 (Mountain rescue/Ashley Cooper pics), 224 (Books/incamerastock); Corbis pp50 (Portrait of woman/Oliver Rossi), 50 (Man with curly hair/Norbert Schaefer), 78 (Fair Isle/Ocean), 96 (ASIMO robot/Everett Kennedy Brown/epa), 114 (Dancing couple/Roy Botterell), 124 (Family ice skating/Altrendo/Juice Images), 126 (Novak Djokovic/Christian Liewig/Liewig Media Sports), 130 (Victoria Pendleton/Gerry Penny/epa), 176 (Pharmacist), 226 (Business speech/Eric Audras/PhotoAlto); Getty Images pp28 (Family in 1974/Victor Drees), 34 (Paul McCartney and John Lennon/Robert Whitaker), 38 (Couple in café/Hugh Sitton), 106 (Cinema audience/Emmanuel Faure), 190 (News broadcast/Kim Steele), 208 (Couple in park/Westend61); Kobal Collection p110 (*Law and Order Special Victims Unit*/Universal TV); OUP pp44 (Woman on public transport/Brand X Pictures), 46 (Well-dressed man/PhotoAlto), 50 (Portrait of man), 50 (Teen boy in park/i love images), 50 (Woman/Mike Stone), 50 (Friends socialising/BananaStock), 54 (Paint roller and tray/Ingram), 54 (Paint/Ingram), 54 (Screwdriver/Dennis Kitchen Studio, Inc.), 60 (Man smiling/Zen Shui), 60 (Businesswoman/Fuse), 60 (Woman smiling/Photodisc), 60 (Woman/Westend61), 60 (Man at desk/Asia Images RF), 62 (Student/Digital Vision), 66 (Elderly woman/Eyebyte), 66 (Student/Blend Images), 76 (Plane at airport/Sergiy Serdyuk), 92 (Phone/Photodisc), 92 (Friends with mobile phone/Cultura), 92 (Telephone receiver/Photodisc), 132 (Picnic basket/Photodisc), 168 (Office/Brand X Pictures), 172 (Woman outside/Gareth Boden), 188 (Business speech/Comstock);

Shutterstock pp60 (Man in locker room/Tomasz Trojanowski), 60 (Man using laptop/wavebreakmedia ltd).

Illustrations by:

Richard Duszczak pp 16-17, 64, 142, 216;
Chris Pavely pp 154-155, 246;
Peters and Zabrasky pp 90-91;
Willie Ryan pp 48, 52, 80.

NOTES